JOYCE RUPP

Essential Writings

Selected with an Introduction by
MICHAEL LEACH

ORBIS BOOKS
Maryknoll, New York 10545

ORBIS BOOKS
Maryknoll, New York 10545

Fathers and Brothers
MARYKNOLL™

Founded in 1970, Orbis Books endeavors to publish works that enlighten the mind, nourish the spirit, and challenge the conscience. The publishing arm of the Maryknoll Fathers and Brothers, Orbis seeks to explore the global dimensions of the Christian faith and mission, to invite dialogue with diverse cultures and religious traditions, and to serve the cause of reconciliation and peace. The books published reflect the views of their authors and do not represent the official position of the Maryknoll Society. To learn more about Maryknoll and Orbis Books, please visit our website at www.maryknollsociety.org.

Library of Congress Cataloging-in-Publication Data

Names: Rupp, Joyce, author. | Leach, Michael, 1940- editor.
Title: Essential writings / Joyce Rupp ; selected with an introduction by Michael Leach.
Description: Maryknoll : Orbis Books, 2017. | Series: Modern spiritual masters series
Identifiers: LCCN 2016041668 (print) | LCCN 2017004850 (ebook) (print) | LCCN 2017004850 (ebook) | ISBN 9781626982338 (pbk.) | ISBN 9781608336982 (e-book)
Subjects: LCSH: Spirituality—Christianity. | Spirituality—Catholic Church.
Classification: LCC BV4501.3 .R863 2017 (print) | LCC BV4501.3 (ebook) | DDC 242—dc23
LC record available at https://lccn.loc.gov/2016041668

For Lester Rupp,
farmer, father, friend

Writing

I wait out sluggish days,
empty evenings, mulish
attempts to capture words
hiding themselves
inside the undulating sea
of my mental thesaurus,
not even remotely available
for me to scoot them
onto my fingers and
into necessary revision.

So I wait, and wait,
and wait some more
while I fumble uselessly
with worthless concoctions
until

one early dawn
the tide comes in
and the first word peeks out.

then they all follow,
and like a flock of gulls
I swoop in to snatch
the sea's latest prey.

—*Joyce Rupp*

Contents

Acknowledgments

This book, which honors and holds up the writings of Joyce Rupp, would not have been possible without the generosity of Tom Grady, president and publisher of Ave Maria Press, whose dedication to his author Joyce Rupp and her community, the Servants of Mary, is an exemplar for all publishers. Just as important has been the expertise and work-beyond-job description of Maria Angelini, Orbis Books Production Manager, who guided and encouraged this editor every step of the way. And a big thanks, too, to Ivy Kelly who played no small role in typing without error a good part of the beautiful writings that follow. This book is blessed.

—*Michael Leach, Editor*

Sources and Abbreviations

Cosmic Dance	*The Cosmic Dance: An Invitation to Experience Our Oneness.* Art by Mary Southard (Maryknoll, NY: Orbis Books, 2002).
Cup of Life	*The Cup of Our Life: A Guide to Spiritual Growth* (Notre Dame, IN: Sorin Books, 1997).
Dear Heart	*Dear Heart, Come Home: The Path of Midlife Spirituality* (New York: Crossroad, 1996).
Fly	*Fly While You Still Have Wings: And Other Lessons My Resilient Mother Taught Me* (Notre Dame, IN: Sorin Books, 2015).
Fragments	*Fragments of Your Ancient Name: 365 Glimpses of the Divine for Daily Meditation* (Notre Dame, IN: Sorin Books, 2011).
Goodbyes	*Praying Our Goodbyes: A Spiritual Companion Through Life's Losses and Sorrows* (Notre Dame, IN: Ave Maria Press, 2009).
May I Dance	*May I Have This Dance? An Invitation to Faithful Prayer Throughout the Year* (Notre Dame, IN: Ave Maria Press, 2007).
My Soul	*My Soul Feels Lean: Poems of Loss and Restoration* (Notre Dame, IN: Sorin Books, 2013).
NCRL	*National Catholic Rural Life Newsletter,* "Let the Land Teach Us" (February 23, 2000).
Ordinary	*Out of the Ordinary: Prayers, Poems, and Reflections for Every Season,* Tenth Anniver-

	sary Edition (Notre Dame, IN: Ave Maria Press, 2010).
Prayer	*Prayer* (Maryknoll, NY: Orbis Books, 2007).
Sophia	*Prayers to Sophia: Deepening Our Relationship with Holy Wisdom* (Notre Dame, IN: Sorin Books, 2010).
Star	*The Star in My Heart: Discovering Inner Wisdom* (Notre Dame, IN: Sorin Books, 2010).
U.S. Catholic	*U.S. Catholic Magazine*, "Desperately Seeking Sophia" (July 2008).
Walk	*Walk in a Relaxed Manner: Life Lessons from the Camino* (Maryknoll, NY: Orbis Books, 2005).

About Joyce Rupp

Joyce Rupp was born on June 8, 1943, in Cherokee, IA, the third of eight children to Lester Rupp and Hilda Wilberding Rupp. She and her siblings grew up working with their parents on a small family farm. They raised cattle, pigs, and chickens and harvested corn, oats, and alfalfa. Joyce's brother Dave, who was next to her in age, died of drowning when he was twenty-three. This was a life-changing event for Joyce. She later wrote about grieving in her bestselling book *Praying Our Goodbyes*.

Joyce entered the Servants of Mary religious community (Servites) at age nineteen after a year in college. She took her first vows in 1964 and received her BA in Elementary Education in 1965 from Duchesne College in Omaha. In 1975 she received an MRE from the University of St. Thomas in Houston. After completing studies in spirituality at Creighton University and the University of Notre Dame, she furthered her interest in Jungian psychology at Naropa University in Boulder, Colorado, for two years, and earned a MTP from the Institute of Transpersonal Psychology, Palo Alto, CA, in 1993.

Sr. Joyce Rupp first taught in elementary schools, was a catechetical consultant to five rural parishes in western Iowa, and served as a volunteer in Appalachia. As associate vocation director for the Archdiocese of Omaha she began giving spiritual retreats to high school and college-age students in 1973. Soon she was leading retreats for adults. Her spiritual direction ministry began to spread in 1980, and Joyce published her first book, *Fresh Bread*, in 1985.

Joyce Rupp soon became widely known for her work as a writer, a spiritual "midwife," and an international retreat and conference speaker. She has led retreats throughout North America and in Europe, Africa, Australia, New Zealand, and Asia. Her twenty-three books have been published throughout the English-speaking world and translated into seven languages.

Her books have won awards from the National Catholic Press Association, the Independent Booksellers Association, and *Spirituality and Health* magazine. In 1994 the trade journal *Publishers Weekly* named Joyce Rupp one of the top ten bestselling Catholic authors in the United States. In 2004 she received the U.S. Catholic Award for Furthering the Cause of Women in the Church for her significant role as a "midwife" for women's spirituality.

In 2008, together with Sr. Margaret Stratman, Joyce founded and became a codirector of The Institute of Compassionate Presence. She has long been a volunteer for hospice and a minister to the dying and their families. Joyce resides in Des Moines, IA, a few hours' drive from what was once the family farm.

Introduction: The Farmer's Daughter

Joyce Rupp is a farmer's daughter, a sister to seven, a Sister to many. She is a planter, grower, and spiritual midwife. She walks hundreds of miles a year and flies thousands more to answer the call of the wild and visit the sick in rich cities and small towns where Main Street often looks like an abandoned movie set. She is a writer, speaker, and retreat giver who receives invitations from five continents. Her books have been published in seven languages, including Croatian and Indonesian. She sings both chants and golden oldies, teaches theology and practices transpersonal psychology, is a lifelong Catholic appreciated by people of all faiths and criticized by some in her own faith as *out there*. Indeed, Joyce is so far out there she is smack dab in the middle of where it's all at.

The purpose of this book is to show you where Joyce is at, where she came from and where she is going, who she is, what she is like, and what she knows for sure. All in her own words.

Here is how Joyce described herself to the editors of *U.S. Catholic* magazine in an April 2000 interview:

> *I always ask people to introduce me as a farmer's daughter, because the older I get and the longer I write, the more I see that my writing really comes out of my roots on the farm. I am very wedded to the earth; that's where I find a lot of spiritual connectedness, with nature. This morning in my hotel room, I tried to "pray the city," and I found that difficult. I'm not a city person. I particularly find a lot of wisdom from the earth from having grown up in the Midwest with the four seasons. It's taught me a*

lot about the cycle of transformation, seeing that whole process of life-death-life.

I call myself a "spiritual midwife" because I see myself not as the person who does the growing for someone else but as nurturing, energizing, being a catalyst, caring for, and affirming the person in the growth process. I help them to know how to nurture and care for themselves just as a midwife would do in helping a woman prepare to give birth.

I once asked Joyce if she watched the TV show *Call the Midwife*. "Yes, I used to but I got tired of all the moaning, screaming, pushing, and crying out." Joyce knew at an early age that there was a time to be born and a time to die. She witnessed siblings and calves come to life, experienced the joy and pain of growth, and learned that love and loss were as certain as seasons of abundance and times of drought. It was her parents reverence for life and their love of the land that planted the seeds of her budding spirituality.

* * *

The first part of this book, *Home*, is a selection of Joyce's writings that reveal this flowering. "Mom was a wonderful gardener," she told me, "and taught me how to help things grow. To this day I am enthralled with seeds and the potential they hold. Dad taught me about farming, about the responsibility of caring for the land and the trust it takes to do the hard work involved in growing crops. Our life revolved around the planting and harvesting seasons, the eternal concern of whether storms would damage the plants, if there would be enough rain or too much rain, if it held off until the hay was baled, and whether or not the corn would be dry for combining before the first snow. I saw how my parents got up early in the morning and didn't stop until it was nearly sundown. The cycle of planting, weeding crops, and harvesting the grain became an inherent part of my being. I never gave much thought to it. I was *in* it."

It wasn't a leap for Joyce to go from tending the earth to accompanying people on their journey through suffering. "The spiritual life," she says, "is a journey toward becoming whole, a day-to-day movement of continually growing into the person we are meant to be."

I asked Macrina Wiederkehr, a Benedictine sister who has been Joyce's friend and kindred spirit for thirty-five years about Joyce's mode of being in the world. "I truly believe," she told me, "that Joyce's ministry of compassion flows out of her communion with the earth which began in Iowa.

"Joyce is a walker," she continued. "She has walked her way into compassion for the earth and for the world. Earth is her teacher. Trees, flora, rocks, mountains, and fields are her counselors. She never allows fear to inhibit her love for adventure and exploration into new paths and new ideas.

"She's full of surprises. Perhaps one of the greatest surprises for me was when we were at a cabin on a writing-vacation and she decided to sleep in a deer hunter's stand so she could be closer to the night sky and see the stars. Sleeping in a deer stand is a metaphoric action that speaks volumes about her spirituality. It takes a disciplined spirit to spend a windy night in a deer stand. It also takes a lover of earth. She has an innate awareness of the medicinal qualities of nature and has been beautifully obedient to this inborn knowledge.

"If I were to ponder three phrases that describe Joyce Rupp's life they would be: she who walks with wild things and learns from them; she who sleeps in deer stands; and she who is always there for you."

The charism of Joyce's religious community, the Servites, is compassion. Their mentor is Mary, mother of sorrows, standing at the foot of the cross. "My interest in compassion took deep root when I entered the community," Joyce said. "My vocation took me to many parts of the earth and brought me close to people who suffer. My understanding deepened in my fifties when I studied transpersonal psychology at Naropa, the Buddhist university in Colorado. I learned about Buddhism's approach to compassion, its dedication to loving kindness. I returned determined to live this essential Christian virtue as fully as I could." Years later Joyce together with Sr. Margaret Stratman designed the Institute of Compassionate Presence.

The second part of this book, *Earth*, highlights some of Joyce's adventures with nature and how she has come to express compassion for all living things, squirrels and snakes and people, the good, the bad, and the ugly. One of her posts at www.joycerupp.com says it like only she can say it:

> *One summer day I sat on the back porch fully immersed in preparing a talk for a conference on "listening to God." As I leaned over my notebook, I heard a bird singing a penetrating, melodious song. The warbling went on and on, but I didn't bother to look or listen because I was concentrating on my work. Finally, an inner stirring drew me to put my pen down. I thought, "Listen! Stop what you are doing! Pay attention to this beautiful song. It is too glorious to miss." I looked up to find the source of the singing and saw a female house-finch seated at the bird feeder and a male finch perched on a branch nearby. The mail finch was singing to the female who pretended to peck at the food, seemingly ignoring the enticing song. Finally, the female lifted up and flew away. The moment she left, the other bird's beautiful music stopped.*
>
> *I thought, "God is always singing a love song, desiring to get my attention, wanting to let me know I am cherished, but I get absorbed in pecking and cleaning. Only by listening to the melody of God will I recognize and respond to what is beneath. Only then will I turn my heart more fully to the One who calls insistently to me."*

Joyce listens for the music of God and her soul moves to a divine dance. She is able to

> *lean back in memory and catch a hint of what I knew long ago when I was a small child living on a farm in rural Iowa. It is the melody of the cosmic dance playing in my soul since those early days, a song that has never stopped singing in me. . . .*
>
> *As I grew older eventually I made some startling discoveries—three of them—and they have changed my life forever. The first of these is the amazing revelation that I am made up of stardust, that every part and parcel of who I am materially was once a piece of a star shining in the heavens. The second discovery is that the air I breathe is the air that has circled the globe and been drawn in and out by people, creatures and vegetation in lands and seas far away. But the most astounding discovery that both awakened and affirmed my early childhood awareness is the fact that I am part of a vast and marvelous dance that goes on unceasingly at every moment in the most minute particles of the universe. (The Cosmic Dance)*

Joyce's spiritual journey began in Iowa, branched far beyond it, then reached for the stars. Her study of world religions enriched her faith and expanded her vision. She became, in my view, what psychiatrist Thomas Hora calls a "beneficial presence in the world," one who endeavors to see the Christ in others and, without trying, brings out what is good and beautiful in them.

Joyce came to realize that "nothing can separate us from the love of Christ" (Romans 8:39), not death, not sin, not anything. Just as a sunbeam can never be separated from the sun or from any other sunbeam, nothing can separate us from the one Light or from each other.

In *God's Enduring Presence* Joyce reflects on Mary's visit to her cousin Elizabeth when Jesus nestled in Mary's womb:

Elizabeth's utter amazement at the presence of the God-Child in Mary calls us to be equally astounded at everyone who comes into our life because each one is also a bearer of God's presence, although that presence might be hidden from easy recognizance. Every person, no matter how mean or ugly-behaving, no matter how obnoxious or unsavory, no matter how irritating or unkind, has something of God within them, even though the divine presence is concealed from our view.

We are undoubtedly aware of people "out there" in whom we find it troublesome to welcome the Christ, such as murderers, drug dealers, sexual predators. But, in reality, the Christ in those near to us can also be difficult to welcome. This person might be someone who interrupts our TV program or who barges into our workplace with some absurd or unnecessary problem. It might be a spouse who insists on having his way or a telemarketer who won't take "no" for an answer. The person might even be a grandparent who fails to echo Elizabeth's welcoming words when her teenage grandchild comes to visit bearing a pierced tongue and tattooed arms.

O Divinity in Disguise, open my eyes and heart to welcome you with the joy that Elizabeth welcomed your presence.

The third part of this book, *Cosmos*, reveals Joyce's emerging consciousness of our inseparable union with God and each other in an amazing universe whose Alpha and Omega is the living Christ.

Joyce Rupp has always sought answers to the question, "What's it all about?" The search led her to see the universe as through a kaleidoscope—that wonderful child's toy you hold to the light to see beauty and harmony unfold. As the kaleidoscope circles, tiny bits and pieces of colored glass twist and turn and come dashing and crashing to the center to form new and beautiful designs. Each design is new, each is different, yet somehow all are the same. The center is Christ—or God or Yahweh or Allah or the Most High, whatever you choose to name the One who draws all dappled things together, and makes all things new.

The stars spin and people sin and the kaleidoscope turns but the Light remains the same. It is the same yesterday, today, and tomorrow. To grow is to change but to look for the One, and see the face of Christ in everyone.

"It is within the brokenness of our humanity that we speak of the Holy One," writes Joyce. "Each glimpse allows us a step further on the bridge uniting us with this eternal goodness. Each name enhances our relationship with the One who exists as the underpinning of our love" (*Fragments of Your Ancient Name*).

When Joyce discovers God as "Deepest Good," she writes this prayer:

> When I sort through the layered texture
> Of what clutters and claims my spirit,
> I find you, Deepest Good, in residence.
> You shine like a piece of gold inside of me.
> In that tranquil, secluded district of soul
> I discover my true, unblemished nature.
> Teach me that there is much more to me
> Than just my struggle and my failure.
> Absorb me in the jewel of your love
> Until I am fully one with your goodness.

The fourth part of this book, *God*, presents a bouquet of names of the Holy One that are like bits of colored glass in the kaleidoscope. The jewel that Joyce's eye fixes on is Sophia, or Wisdom. How fitting that at the end of this book Compassion meets Wisdom, and they are one.

* * *

There is no fifth part, so let's take this moment to see Joyce Rupp up close and personal. Her writings reveal a wise and bouncy old soul but to paraphrase Anthony Quinn who said of Peter O'Toole as *Lawrence of Arabia*: "She is *not* perfect."

Joyce will be the first to tell you, as she does often enough on these pages, that she is an overly responsible woman who works too hard. And, like you and me, she gets tired, sad, and depressed. One of my favorite of her poems is *Shabby and Awkward:*

> Shabby and awkward,
> spiritually disheveled,
> I run in pursuit
> of taming my untruths.
>
> Finally I fall
> into the ragged gutter
> of those endless struggles,
> unable to keep pushing
> toward unmet goals.
>
> Only then
> does the dross disappear,
> only then
> does the lame get up
> and walk.

Joyce's compassion runs like gold through a mountain chain in all her highs and lows. Everyone who knows her has a story like her Servite sister Ginny Silvestri: "When my mother died, Joyce immediately flew from Des Moines to Detroit where my family and I were gathered for the funeral. Joyce was helpful and attentive to us in many ways, but what I will always be most grateful for was her willingness to give the reflection for the funeral liturgy. The evening before the funeral, she sat with my siblings and me very late into the night and listened to us share stories about our mom. At liturgy the next morning, she incorporated our stories and our feelings into her reflection very beautifully and sensitively. It was a wonderful gift to my family and an expression of friendship to me that I still treasure."

Paula D'Arcy, founder of The Red Bird Foundation, treasures a small moment when Joyce was there for her: "Joyce was participating in the walking pilgrimage I co-lead from Paris to Chartres. On the last day, the best and most beautiful day of walking, when we're about to enter Chartres as a group, with the bells ringing in the tower of Chartres cathedral, one of the walkers was struggling to keep up. My co-leader went ahead to lead the group, and I stayed behind to walk with the woman who was struggling, knowing that I was missing the joy of walking in with everyone after three long days of anticipation. And suddenly there was Joyce at my side, having decided to stay with me. You do not forget such moments and such gestures of love."

What I remember most about Joyce is the weekend she stayed at our house before giving a retreat at Maryknoll, forty miles away. Saturday night Vickie and I took her to see *Jersey Boys* on Broadway. I've never seen someone have so much fun at a Broadway show other than myself. At the end the Jersey Boys run through some of their greatest hits and ask the audience to sing with them. Nobody in the audience sang with more joy or more in tune than Joyce! She clapped her hands and swayed her hips and knew the words to every song. "Big Girls Don't Cry." "Walk Like a Man." "My Boyfriend's Back." "Rag Doll." "Can't Take My Eyes off of You." I had never pictured Joyce as a teenager before. But there she was.

We had a lot of fun doing five books over the years, including one of her favorites *The Cosmic Dance* with stunning artwork by our mutual friend Sr. Mary Southard. Bob Hamma, editor at her primary publishing house, Ave Maria Press, observed what I, too, experienced: "I've learned so much from working with Joyce through the years—about prayer, gratitude, and keeping things in perspective."

Joyce's greatest gift to the universe, in my view, is her presence. She comes in a small package and speaks in a soft voice, but her presence can be felt a thousand miles away.

I wish I had saved the e-mails Joyce sent me when I was taking care of my aging parents in Chicago, flying back and forth, dealing with their needs and emotions, when at the same time Alzheimer's disease invaded my spouse Vickie's brain. Joyce's e-mails never preached. Her words were simple. They picked me up when I was down.

Joyce Rupp will be most remembered by those who weren't blessed to know her up close and personal for her writings—on home, the earth, the stars in heaven, and God in each of us. This book is our gift to you.

—*Michael Leach*

1

Home

Is this heaven?
No, it's Iowa.
—Ray Kinsella in Field of Dreams

Where we love is home—
home that our feet may leave, but not our hearts.
—Oliver Wendell Holmes, Sr.

There's no place like home.
—Dorothy in Wizard of Oz

Joyce Rupp embodies Iowa. In her walk, her talk, her mode of being in the world. On a clear day in Iowa you really can see forever. You behold the horizon in every direction and your mind stretches and your heart aches for the mystery beyond. If you look long enough, and listen hard enough, you realize anything is possible.

Here Joyce lays bare what is was like to grow up with hard-working parents and seven siblings on a poor Iowa farm. She shows us what it was like to first experience the joys and pains of being human, to seek meaning in young adulthood and midlife, to say goodbye and come to listen for the divine hello. She gives a clue to what it means to "come back home."

By the end of this book you will see what she has come to see, what T. S. Eliot knew: "We shall not cease from exploration, and the end of all our exploring will be to arrive where we started and know the place for the first time."

THE FIRST TIME

imagine the first time
you opened your eyes
and saw a human face
imagine the first time
you touched your hands
and felt the softness
imagine the first time
you heard the sound
of your own name
imagine the first time
you looked at a flower
and smelled the fragrance
imagine the first time
you walked on your own
and didn't fall down
imagine the first time
you had a delicious bath,
warm and sudsy
imagine your first drink of water
your first ray of sunshine
your first time in a park
your first look at the moon
now take it all in again
as if today
is your last day . . .

—*Cosmic Dance*, 39

ABBA

Mark 14:36

Abba, father, kind parent, gentle daddy.
Strength balanced with a caring concern.
A trusted lap in the early years of childhood.
An inner, assuring voice to be counted on.
Guiding hand of love held forth for confidence.
The deliberate stance of ready protection.
No wonder Jesus chose to call you Abba

Knowing he could lean on you for stamina.
He needed you every step of the way.
And so do I.
Today: I lean on the strength of *Abba*.

—*Fragments*, January 11

THE GIFT MY FATHER GAVE ME

*At a certain point you say
to the woods, to the sea, to the mountains, the world,
Now I am ready.
Now I will stop and be wholly attentive.
You empty yourself and wait, listening . . .*
—*Annie Dillard*

I learned how to be aware when I was young. I saw how my father would watch the skies for storms, how he sensed when it was the right time to plant and to harvest. He taught me how to sniff the air and smell the seasons, to look at winter skies and know when snow was about to land. I learned what hail clouds looked like in the spring and which clouds would bring the rain. It was Dad who talked about being able to hear the corn grow in the summer and who noticed how the maple leaves turned when a change was on its way. He was attentive to the farm animals and knew when they needed special care. I watched him find the places where fish and turtles swam in local creeks and how he ran his hand through the grain as it filled the bins at harvest time.

Awareness was a great gift my father gave me. I did not know in those early years what a vital component of life I had learned. As I grew older I forgot how essential it is to be alert and attentive to what is a part of my life. It has taken me time to recover this gift and I still lose it now and again. I am growing in awareness, however, and each day I re-commit myself to this gift as I turn my entire being toward the cosmic dance of life, longing to lean into it with all I am and all I do.   —*Cosmic Dance*, 31, 32–33

MOTHER

How wide is your womb of extensive love.
How full your breasts of inner nurturance.
How caressing the vast arms of your caring.
How precious your storehouse of wisdom.
Mother, you clothe us with needed courage.
You protectively shield our self from harm,
Drawing us near to you when we are afraid.
You never doubt our merit and worth,
Even when we are doubting it ourselves.
You are the welcome we'll always receive.

Today: I am held in the arms of *Mother*.
                                   —*Fragments*, January 14

THE GIFT MY MOTHER GAVE ME

Not until I was an adult did I know how much Mom enjoyed dancing. She told me about this one day when she found it difficult to get out of her chair due to stiff arthritic limbs. She followed that comment about dancing with, "Aunt Ida told me: 'Hilde, you'll be dancing into heaven.' I wonder what she'd think if she saw me now."

Mom's fondness for country life and the delight she experienced there in her younger years strengthened her durable nature. When she married, she not only endured the financial struggles and relentless hard work, she took pride in the abundance of her large garden. She also tried to help us enjoy the farm. When they stopped raising brooder chickens, Mom took the time and energy to clean out that small building and create a playhouse for my older sister and me. She looked back on that time with satisfaction and said, "I think I enjoyed doing that as much as you girls did." She also gave us all kinds of suggestions for games we could play in the grove. In the midst of hardship, my mother chose to seek joy and bring it to others whenever she could. —*Fly*, 33

ALL STRUGGLE IS NOT LOSS

My parents lived on rented land where Dad grew alfalfa, corn, and oats, while also raising cattle and pigs. Along with giving birth to eight children, Mom took care of cooking, laundry, cleaning, gardening and canning produce, childcare, sewing and mending, mowing a huge lawn, cow-milking, chicken-raising, and keeping the farm's financial ledgers.

The old two story, wooden-framed house that she and Dad moved into consisted of three bedrooms, a kitchen, and a living room. My brothers slept in one upstairs bedroom and we girls in the other. In summertime, the boys learned to exist with their buzzing companions, a hive of honey bees that took over a spot under the eaves.

Each day required constant labor. There was no indoor plumbing, and the youngest babies all wore cloth diapers. These smelly things had to be rinsed out in a bucket of water ("the diaper pail"), then washed in a hand-wringer tub and hung outdoors to dry. If any clothing required pressing, this was done with an iron heated on the top of the stove. And then there was feeding the family. Besides produce from a huge garden, Mom used every item of food available. Each summer she sent us older children to the nearby grove of trees to pick fruit from wild elderberry and chokecherry bushes. From these she produced delicious jellies and jams.

Inconvenience and privations abounded. One of these involved drinking water. A windmill in the pasture pumped water from the well into a pipe leading to a faucet south of the big red barn. That's where Mom walked, through a manure-laden cattle yard, to carry buckets of drinking water back to the house. If there was no wind, water from the well would not flow. Sometimes this proved disastrous, like the day she cooked a meal for the five men helping my father with the harvesting. This turned out to be one of the few times my mother fell apart, her inner mettle totally spent.

While Mom prepared the noon meal for these men, she ran out of cooking and drinking water. This presented an awful dilemma because there was no one to watch the three of us children, all under the age of six. She couldn't take us with her through the mucky cattle-yard but she had to get the water. "Finally, I just said a prayer, left Jerry (the oldest child) to watch you two, got the buckets and hurried down there. I couldn't believe it. Right when I got to the faucet, the wind stopped blowing. No water. I just stood there and cried."

It wasn't only drinking water that was hard to get. Water for washing clothes, bathing, and cleaning dishes came from a rain-water cistern next to the house. Priming the pump demanded a significant amount of pushing and pulling on the handle at the top of the cistern before water streamed forth.

There was, of course, no indoor plumbing. In frigid, winter weather, those trips to the outhouse felt twice as long. Besides this icy inconvenience, overnight chamber pots in the house needed emptying in the outhouse the next morning.

There were other household chores that were equally burdensome. The stove was fueled on corn cobs that had to be hauled in from their storage bins in a corner of the garage. The dirty, black coal that fired the living room stove came in huge chunks that had to be broken down in order to fit inside. With this endless stream of work and responsibilities, I wonder how my mother ever found time to sew. She proved to be an excellent seamstress, one of her proudest achievements being the stylish blue suit she made for herself. Since she couldn't afford to buy new material, she took apart one of my father's suits that no longer fit him and used that cloth instead.

When Mom was thirty-seven, she experienced an especially tough year. While still living in the century-old house, she was pregnant with a seventh child. This proved to be one of her most difficult pregnancies with several overnight stays in the hospital before the actual birth. A day after one of those times of hemorrhaging and pain, her father died of blood poisoning. She was too weak to attend the funeral, but in spite of how ill she felt, visitors who came for the funeral found hospitality and lodging at our home, along with meals that Mom prepared for them. It was during this year, too, that Dad caught his finger in a grain grinder that cut the end off of it. This led to a serious infection.

Mom must have struggled greatly as she faced those constant hardships. Yet, she did not give in to self-pity or resentment. She picked herself up and went on, day after day, year after year. In *Scarred by Struggle, Transformed by Hope*, Joan Chittister writes, "All struggle is not loss. All those who struggle do not give way to depression, to death of the spirit, to dearth of heart. We not only can survive struggle but, it seems, we are meant to survive in new ways, with new insights, with new heart." It was not so much "a new heart" being created in my mother. Instead, a basic resilience deepened and a spirit that refused to let go of hope for better days became stronger.

—*Fly*, 28–31

THE CUP OF LIFE

Every time you listen with great attentiveness to the voice that calls you the Beloved, you will discover within yourself a desire to hear that voice longer and more deeply. —*Henri J. M. Nouwen*

Like my other siblings, I had chores to do after school. Mine consisted of feeding the chickens and gathering the eggs. I didn't like doing this because my free spirit wanted to be out in the grove playing or down by the creek watching tadpoles and catching minnows.

But one day all of that changed for me. I learned that I had a secret companion who always kept me company, even when I was doing the daily farm chores. Hidden away deep within my heart was a loving being named God who would always love me and would never leave me. It was at this time that a wise teacher taught me about friendship with God. She assured me that I would never be alone because I was carrying the very life of God within me. I was enthused about this discovery. I could sense that "Someone" was there. I began carrying on endless conversations with this Friend. Walking home from school, doing my chores, playing in the grove—all of these activities became opportunities to be with my "special Someone." This was the beginning of my relationship with God.

As I grew older, I recognized this inner presence as a dynamic source of guidance and consolation. I became ever more deeply rooted in the belief that this indwelling God loves me totally and unconditionally. To this day, I draw comfort and courage from the belief that I am a container holding the presence of God. This awesome and humbling gift of the Divine Indwelling constantly enlivens my spiritual path and seeds my transformation.

The more I become aware of God's presence in my life, the more I thirst to know this Sacred One at an ever deeper and deeper level. Like a cup that seemingly has more and more room to be filled, so I feel that my capacity to be united with God keeps expanding. The more I know how loved I am by God (the more my cup is filled), the more I am always thirsting for more of God (seeing how much room the cup still has in it to receive).

When I think about the spiritual life, I think of a life with God that is healthy and vibrant. The root and foundation of this life is *relationship*. This relationship may have many struggles, crooked paths, and hidden corners, but at the core, there is a

bond that is deep and strong. This relationship feeds and nour-
ishes my inner self and gives a vitality and vibrancy to all of my
life. Each one of us is a temple of the Holy One.

Each of us carries a spiritual power in us that can cause even
the tiniest of faith-seeds to grow. It is vital that we protect and
nurture this relationship so that it thrives. The cup of our spiritual life must be cared for and replenished as it pours its contents away in loving service. Like the cup with its boundaries,
we, too, need parameters so that our life does not seep away into
endless busy-ness and unguarded, unfocused activity.

—*Cup of Life*, 11–12

A DEATH IN THE FAMILY

It was 1968. I had never thought about anyone in my family
dying. I was young and they all seemed so full of life. Then came
the phone call and my sister's voice saying, "I am so sorry to
have to be the one to tell you. We lost Dave today. . . ." My
twenty-three year-old brother, the one next in age to me, had
drowned. Dave was the one I dearly loved and had yearned
to know better. The memory of our last time together flashed
through my mind: Dave, sitting in the easy chair smiling at me,
and I, feeling a kind of sadness because we had so much yet
to learn and to share with one another. Our time together had
seemed all too short. Strange how I remember the exact words
and know precisely what I was doing at the moment when the
phone rang. The shock of that message deeply embedded the
details in my memory.

The painful truth of how hard it is to say goodbye started to
root itself and take hold in my heart. As I look back, I feel as
though I have had this book [*Praying Our Goodbyes*] in my soul
for a long, long time. While it is a book about farewell to our
loved ones who have died, it is also about many other forms of
goodbye in our lives, all those events and experiences in which
we feel a deep sense of loss. I believe that instead of running
from these goodbyes, we need to take the time to reflect upon

them, to "pray them." In doing so we can become wiser, deeper and more compassionate.

Although life is difficult and always has its share of sorrows, life is also very good and deeply enriching. It holds many promises of growth and treasures of joy. It is not easy to believe this when we are hurting greatly because of our loss. Sometimes it takes years to understand and accept this truth. That is how it has been for me.

The grief of losing my brother touched numerous areas of my life. I found myself fighting, avoiding, struggling with and being angry or confused about the many forms of goodbye that I experienced: being uprooted from one place to another, deaths of family friends and a dear uncle, termination of a significant friendship of many years, betrayal by one I had really trusted, struggles with church changes and with religious life decisions. Always the inner question "Why me?" accompanied any deep hurt or demands to let go. I kept asking, "Why should I experience the hard things in life when I am trying my best to be good?" I also had an angry "Not me!" and a pitiable "Poor me!" that rose up inside my aching spirit. Over the years I developed an attitude that said life was always supposed to be a continuous hello. The hurt and wrenching ache of goodbye was not supposed to be there.

Eventually I accepted the fact that life is unfair at times, that it has its share of difficulties no matter how good I am or how much I am yearning for happiness. I began to realize that I could become a more whole human being because of the way that life sometimes pressed painfully against my happiness and my deep desire to have everything go well. I know that although I will sometimes feel broken apart or empty, eventually I will mend and be filled again.

Loss will never be easy for me, but I am much better at identifying the need to let go and at understanding the call to move on as a means of growth. Sometimes goodbyes still overwhelm me, but my questions are changing. Instead of asking "Why me?" I much more readily ask "How?"—How can I move gracefully through the ache of the farewells that come into my life? I also ask "Who?"—Who will be with me in this process?—because I know that I cannot go through intense leave-takings without some kinship and some loving support to sustain me.

These new questions have grown in my consciousness because of a very graced moment several years ago. The reality of my battle with goodbyes finally asserted itself one early morning as I walked across the beautiful University of Notre Dame campus. I found myself on a green lawn, facing a Pieta. The Pieta was shocking to me, stark and harsh, so unlike the soft, curving, feminine touch of Michelangelo's Woman and Son. This Pieta had sharp, angular features. The figures were full of holes. It was a black, metallic affront to my eyes, speaking loudly of suffering, of pain and agony. I could hardly bear to look at it, and I wanted to run away. But something inside of me drew me to sit and keep my eyes focused on the Woman of Sorrows who held her dead Son in her arms. Strong, powerful emotions pushed tears to my eyes. I hated the unfairness of life. I resented it in every fiber of my being. But I felt a deep yearning to discover a truth I had never possessed. As I looked and looked at the depiction of sorrow, the pain of goodbye seared through my gaze. I saw there a tremendous union of love, great strength, coupled with a heart-wrenching moment of lamentation and agony at life's unfairness. Truly this Pieta spoke more deeply the harsh truth of farewell than anything I had ever seen.

Deep within me the words came: "You must face goodbyes. You must come to terms with life's unfairness. You cannot allow your 'poor me's' and 'not me's' to stunt your growth any longer. You need to use your energy to give life, not to fight death." I continued to sit there for a long time.

When I arose, I knew what I had to do. I would walk the path of Jesus in a thirty-day Ignatian retreat, a retreat that takes one into the paschal mystery with its loss and sorrow, its hope and resurrection. I would stop running. I'd throw myself into God's arms and I would ask God all those questions that were forever rising up to choke me. I would spend my days with Jesus: What would he say about life's losses? What was the meaning of his own life and suffering?

That moment of decision was one of the greatest graces of my life. My thirty days with God and a wonderful retreat directress changed my inner focus. So many essential, life-giving wisdoms surfaced during those days: the hello-goodbye pattern as an integral part of all human existence, the necessity of change in order to have growth, and the need to let go before one can truly move on. I also learned that the cost of discipleship is inherent in any following of Jesus and that this following causes choices which mean goodbye to some parts of life and hello to others.

Most important, I discovered that for the Christian, hello always follows goodbye in some form if we allow it. There is, or can be, new life, although it will be different from the life we knew before. The resurrection of Jesus and the promises of God are too strong to have it be any other way.   —*Goodbyes*, xii–xv

RESURRECTION

An unknown Iowa pasture,
two black figures in the dawn,
one large, one very small,
so small as to almost not be seen,
hidden in the fresh folds
of unblemished April grass.

A mother cow gives birth,
leans down, nudges her child,
helps his wobbly legs to stand,
licks away the womb's silk
and offer the fullness of her udder.

Everyday, somewhere,
a new creation.

Everyday, somewhere,
a new life marked with splendor,
leaving behind the unwrapped linens
of an empty womb.

—*My Soul*, 124

MOMENTS OF WOW!

During those years of travel when I was an adult, Mom and I became good friends. Our trips eased her loneliness and fed her thirst for adventure. For at least eight years we journeyed to New England, New York State, Oregon, Washington State, Wisconsin, Illinois, Colorado, Montana, Wyoming, Arkansas, Texas, Missouri, and Hawaii. Certain moments are imprinted on my memory, special ones in which Mom's unassuming delight and open eagerness touched my heart.

Our time in New England remains the most memorable. What sparkling eyes she had when we dined at a quaint restaurant near a Cape Cod shoreline. Later that week she surprised me with her appreciation of beauty when she remarked, "I just love this" as we crossed a picturesque, wooden bridge in the New Hampshire woods. In Vermont, the autumn trees displayed their best colors and she took to saying "Wow!" every time we turned a bend in the road and came across another glorious hillside. Then she got carried away and began greeting the most beautiful views with, "Wow, wow, wow!" Her voice carried such happiness that I joined with her "Wow, wow, wow!" Each time we let out the exclamation, we followed it with a gleeful laugh.

—*Fly*, 80–81

SOUL CONTRACTIONS

My mother ages
all too quickly now,
the latest illness
claiming more chunks

of her vitality each day.
This beloved woman
whose womb held my body,
I now hold
in the chalice of my vigilance.

Sadness and sorrow
pulse inside my spirit,
a kindred soul-contraction
resonating with her spiritual gestation
as she prepares
during these final years
for her birth into eternity.

Dear mother,
I, who burst forth from
your womb
on a sunny morning in June,
embrace you now with gratitude,
praying to let you go freely,
to encourage your spirit

to wing forward peacefully
into the mystery
of the One Great Womb,
where there is space
enough
to embrace us all.

CLIPPED WINGS

How did it come to this?

A forced landing, weakened wings
crippled and cropped with age,
a solid source of former strength,
taking you through
dark clouds and heavy downpours.

Those resilient wings assured your
bodily independence
as you soared through storms,
high winds battering
and pressing upon your life.

Now those same weathered wings
bear evidence of missing feathers,
thinning bones and shrunken wingspan,
no longer able to lift and soar
or glide with the gusto that carried
you through turbulent tempests.

Slowly, slowly you learn to accept
those clipped wings, to be content
with nesting in the arms of elderhood.

You submit to this final appendage
of your journey, bid farewell
to cherished autonomy
and slowly fold your worn wings
in peaceful surrender.

—*Fly*, 135–38

"LET THIS BE MY LAST WORD, THAT I TRUST IN YOUR LOVE"

Mom lived until April 20. This happened to be Holy Thursday, four days before Easter, the hope-filled feast of Jesus being raised from the dead. In mid-morning of that day a call came from my sister-in-law Opal telling me, "The doctor said to notify the children. Mom's not going to make it." Opal explained that the night before Mom had developed severe pain in her left leg which turned out to be a blood clot. True to our mother's history of endurance, she toughed it out that night. The next morning she needed hospitalization and soon after being admitted, her doctor recognized the end was near.

"Happy Easter." These were Mom's last words—the final gift she offered, spoken to Father Gene Sitzmann, a former pastor who came to anoint Mom with the blessed oils for the sick and dying. Although her greeting came out in a weak whisper, it was accompanied with a tender smile. With only a few hours before leaving us behind, she still managed to be gracious and thoughtful to someone else. And she must have recognized her own Easter was near at hand.

Death did not wait long. An hour or so later, Mom departed. Those who were present noticed how peaceful she seemed during those remaining hours of life. Here was the great leave-taking for which Hilda Rupp had readied. With strong faith, she embraced this ending, not fearing what was to be. In *The Heart of God*, Rabindranath Tagore prays, "Let this be my last word, that I trust in Your love." Mom trusted. She went easily into the Holy One's loving embrace. Shortly after Father Sitzmann left, she turned onto her right side and detached from those in the room. Her eyes became riveted, looking beyond into the distance, complete attention given to what those in the room could not behold. Did she see her beloved mother, lost to her for sixty-seven years? Were her husband and son David beckoning? Surely her many deceased friends gathered among those urging her homeward, "Come, come, Hilda, we've been waiting for you."

I'll always be grateful to my sister Lois for asking the hospital staff to wait for my arrival before removing Mom's body. When I walked into the room a half hour after her death, my brother-in-law Jim said, "She's gone." My heart plummeted. Gone? Where? Where are you, Mom? I don't want you *gone*. Not yet. Not now. I went to the bed where my mother's inert body lay, her limbs still warm. She was slightly curled in a cocoon-like position. I stroked her thin, damp hair, held her face in my hands and kissed her goodbye. But this time my mother did not respond.

Silence. Dead. Gone. I tried my utmost to accept that my resilient mother was no longer there. Only later that day did I consider how the empty shell of her body suggested the translucent sheath that a butterfly leaves behind when it takes flight.

Then I recalled a conversation of ours four months earlier. Mom had leaned over the Scrabble board that night and announced, "You know I'm not afraid of dying." I thought, "Where did that come from all of a sudden?" I said out loud, "Well, Mom, I'm really glad to hear that, but I want you around for a long time." She smiled her endearing smile and said with characteristic good humor, "Well, just make sure I have my wings on when I go!"

As if in confirmation that she had gained those fresh wings of freedom, two butterflies flitted by when we turned to leave the cemetery after her funeral several days later. I smiled at the thought of my mother leaving this world with new wings, strong and free, carrying her to a long-awaited destination.

—*Fly*, 167–70

FLY

Fly, fly
while you still
have wings.

Fly with buoyancy.
Do not falter in fervor
or waver in eagerness.

Lift off with a zestful spirit.

Enter fully what remains
of the fleeting,
diminishing years of life.
Do not wait
to follow what the heart
truly desires.

Fly now.

Take yourself
out the door into fresh

freedom.
Celebrate what awaits.
Spend yourself
like there's no tomorrow,

because there may be
no tomorrow.

Open your heart
to receive
latent possibilities of joy
and loving, lasting memories.

Fly, fly, fly,
while you still
have wings.

—Fly, 67–68

I KNOW HOW THE FLOWERS FELT

The rain to the wind said,
"You push and I'll pelt."
They so smote the garden bed
That the flowers actually knelt,
And lay lodged—though not dead.
I know how the flowers felt.

—Robert Frost

If you have ever said a deeply significant goodbye, you know "how the flowers felt," you know what it is like to have life pelt you with sorrow, to be overwhelmed with emptiness, loneliness, confusion and sadness. At these times we are bent over, crushed, like the flowers that "lay lodged—though not dead." The pain is overwhelming, often too deep for tears. The sorrow of it can pervade one's whole self and hurt in every part of one's being. No medicine, no bandage, no diversion, no luxury, no words can assuage the hurt and give it the freedom to desist and cease its painful bending, almost breaking, of the heart. Time and the strength of God's presence can lessen the pain, but even these gifts cannot take the pain away or cure it completely. Just when we think that the last bit of goodbye is out of our heart, we hear someone's name, or we recall a memory, or we have another dream, or we see a house that looks like the one we left, or an old wound of the spirit flares up in our consciousness, and the pain is suddenly very real again.

Every goodbye has some suffering in it, and the greater the parting, the deeper the pain; the greater the loss, the more severe is the empty place that accompanies it. Some of us feel the hurt more than others. So much depends on our personality, our personal history, our God relationship, and our own philosophy of life. People who are deep feeling will usually ache over goodbyes a great deal more than those who approach life on a more intellectual, analytical level. People whose families brush the hurt of loss aside or cover it up with silence, busyness or other ways of avoidance will probably find themselves doing the same thing, not realizing how intense the loss actually is. No matter how we stuff it away or avoid it, however, the pain of goodbyes will show itself in our lives at some time.

I listen to the story of one who has lost a dearly beloved spouse and I wonder if there can be any goodbye so deep as that death in a person's life. I hear the agony of one who has recently been divorced, who has experienced the death of love itself. "Surely," I say to myself, "this goodbye is one of the deepest wounds of all." Then a young man comes into my life, talented and promising, and he suffers a broken neck in a swimming accident, paralyzed for life, forced to say goodbye to many of his dreams for the future. I realize how intense his inner pain is. I meet a man who has been in deep depression because of a forced early retirement. He tells me with tears in his eyes how his whole identity has been that of his work world. He has spent a year struggling with questions about the value of his life and its purpose. It has been a year full of suffering.

The stories go on and on and so does the hurt inherent in them. No two people say goodbye in exactly the same way and

no two people suffer their farewells in the same way, but suffer
they do. That is why the mystery of suffering must be considered
when one is reflecting on the losses in life.

—*Goodbyes*, 15–16

FALSE THEORIES ABOUT SUFFERING

A woman shared with me how she had tried to account for the
pain in her life. She had suffered from osteoporosis for a major
portion of her life and was always hurting, in and out of the hospital with broken bones. One evening she had an opportunity to
go to a faith-healing service. She said to the faith-healer, "I don't
know what I'm doing here; I think God wants me to have this
suffering for a reason." The healer replied, "God doesn't want
you to have this. God wants you to be whole, happy in body,
mind, and spirit." She looked at him in surprise and said, "Well,
if God didn't send this to me, who *can* I blame?"

Who can we blame? If we listen closely to those who hurt or
those who are trying to console someone who hurts, we can hear
in their remarks a certain belief about who causes suffering and
why. Their beliefs usually center around one of the following
reasons: First, God sends the hurt, the bitter loss, because he
loves us so much. Thus, the greater our difficulties, the greater is
God's love for us because suffering is a purification and a means
of transformation. (A sister in my community who had numerous operations for malignant growths was once told: "You must
be loved very specially by God to have been given all of this
suffering." She replied, "Well, then, I wish God didn't love me
so much!") Another belief says that God sends pain because we
are being punished for some sin of the past. There is guilt in this
belief and oftentimes added sorrow because of the feeling that
the sufferers indirectly caused God to send the suffering. They
believe it would not have happened had it not been for their
sin. (A young couple was deeply grieved at the death of their
two-year-old son. When he died, they concluded that God had
taken their child because he was born out of wedlock.) Thirdly,
some think that God sends the suffering to test them, to see if

they really have faith and to prove their love for God in times of trial. Finally, there is a belief that God sends suffering for some reason that we do not understand. People often say, "It is God's will for us and we must simply accept it if we are to be good and faithful followers."

Not one of these four beliefs is an accurate approach for understanding the suffering of our broken places or for living through them. The major premise in all of these beliefs is false. *God does not send suffering to us.* We still have a lot of unhealthy thinking in our theology of suffering. Whenever we say "God sends suffering," we are entering into pagan-tinged territory. In ancient times people also struggled with the ache and pain that came into their human existence. They questioned the elements: Why lightning and storms that destroyed? Why no rain or why too much sun for the crops? Why infertility for some women and not for others? Why death, disease, or other calamities that crippled and stole life?

They began to see all these mysterious struggles as coming from some hidden power in the situation. Something or someone was sending them good or bad things. They developed a theory that, if they appeased the mysterious powers, which they presumed caused good or bad to happen, then they would be spared life's travails and pains. The gods, as these powers were later named, would then be good to them in return and would not send them suffering.

This theology of suffering, based on an appeasement of the gods who had power over them, was carried over into Old Testament stories. Recall the story of Abraham who was asked to kill his only son on the altar of sacrifice to prove his faith in the true God (Gn 22). A messenger of God entered in and stopped Abraham. When this happened a tradition of thought was broken: no more human sacrifices to appease the one true God. It was a breakthrough, but the idea of sacrifices of appeasement persisted for a long, long time as we can see in the New Testament approach that refers to Jesus as being a scapegoat or an appeasement sacrifice to the Father (1 Cor 6:20; 1 Pt 1:19; Heb 10:1–18).

The testing approach to suffering has also been held for many years. In the story of Job, the author tells us that God tested Job by destroying everyone that Job loved and everything of value that Job owned. What kind of God would do this? The author of the Book of Job was struggling with the mystery of suffering just as we do and concluded that God was a testing God.

The thought that God sends suffering as a punishment for our sins is expressed throughout humanity's history, throughout the Old Testament and in the New Testament. When Jesus is with the disciples they ask him about a blind man: "Rabbi, who sinned, this man or his parents, for him to have been born blind?" Jesus answered them, "Neither he nor his parents sinned. He was born blind so that the works of God might be displayed in him" (Jn 9:2–3). At another time Jesus himself raised the same kind of question in order to dispel the theory of suffering as a punishment for sin. When "some people arrived and told him about the Galileans whose blood Pilate had mingled with that of their sacrifices," Jesus said to them, "Do you suppose these Galileans who suffered like that were greater sinners than any other Galileans?

They were not, I tell you" (Lk 13:1–3). In both cases Jesus is refuting the long held belief that the suffering of the man born blind, or of the murdered Galileans or of anyone in a similar position, is a punishment for sin. In each of these circumstances Jesus goes on to point out the necessity of repenting of one's sinfulness and suggests that instances such as these can be invitations for a change of heart or for inner conversion. In doing this, he implies that suffering *can* be an opportunity for us to reflect on our life, the kind of persons we are, how we relate to others, what we value, but Jesus flatly refuses to uphold the traditional theory that suffering is sent as a punishment for one's sins.

What about the will of God? Does God will our suffering? God does not send our suffering or want us to have it, but God does allow it to be there. Jesus himself struggled with the "will of the Father" when he was in his moment of agony (Lk 22:39–46). Jesus was fully human. He did not want the pain. He begged his Father to enter into his goodbye moment and to take away the pain: "Father," he said, "if you are willing, take this cup away from me."

When Jesus continued with "Nevertheless, let your will be done, not mine," he was accepting his painful situation. The Father did not enter in, did not perform a miracle and keep him from the cross; he did not save Jesus from being human. He allowed Jesus to have full participation in the human condition just as all of us have to enter fully into it. God's will for us is that of our happiness, our peace of mind and heart. God does not will us or want us to suffer life's hurts, but God does allow the suffering to happen because, as Rabbi Kushner says so clearly, for God to do otherwise would be to block our human nature and our human condition. Accidents do happen, death does come to us all, disease is prevalent in our world, but God is not *doing* those things to us. We are full and finite human beings living on an earth where natural disasters occur, where genetic conditions exist, where we sometimes make poor or sinful choices, where life does not always work as we had planned and hoped it would. We are blessed and burdened with our humanity, with the mystery of growing into a wholeness of personhood which involves continual goodbyes. We are frail and unfinished, subject always to the possibility of pain.

We live in a world where we know we cannot escape our own mortality, our final goodbye before the eternal hello.

—*Goodbyes*, 19–23

EVANGELISTA

Evangelista, my elderly friend,
a wise woman whose insight
and easy humor stretched me
beyond my youthful perceptions.

Now she's a different person.

One lousy cerebral stroke
has stolen her gentle voice
and captured her creaky limbs.
Soon, it will rob her totally.

Today her thin, frail body
lies motionless on a hospital bed,
IV tube connecting her to fluids
while she dreams the dark sleep
none of us can enter.

I call her name quietly
and welcome the surprising smile
that slides out of her deep slumber,
overjoyed at seeing momentary light
in her grey-blue eyes.
I glimpse for one brief space
the woman she has been,
the one I have loved and admired
for so long.

Soon she surrenders once more
to a place beyond that refuses my visitation.
Little lines of clear drool slip
from the corners of her wrinkled mouth,
her raggedy-doll head lopping over,
a vibrant spirit ebbing from an aged body.

As I sit there sadly musing at what must be
I whisper "Go home" to her imprisoned spirit,
but this body of hers does not listen to me.

After one hundred years
of faithfully housing a soul,
it is not yet ready.

—*My Soul*, 64–65

AT HOME WITH WHO I AM

Letting go was mid-life's central gesture. You let go of people and you let go of expectations, and if you were lucky, you found a way to do it without letting go of hope.
— Elizabeth Kay

she found the skin
lying there
on her front doorstep.

she told me this
in a disgusted voice,
filled with a bit of fear,
said she got the broom
and hastily swept
the skin away.

an unsuspecting snake
slipping out of
a piece of its life,
shedding a shell
of what used to be,
leaving behind
a thin transparent slip
of a former reality.

I thought:
I'd have received that skin
on my doorstep,
a graced moment of calling.
I'd have wondered
at the synchronicity
of its presence.

but then I realized
the turns and tumbles
of my inner life,
and knew that I, too,
have swept many a skin
away from my doorstep
with just as much disgust
and terror.

I always feel called into the mysterious experience of transformation as I join with other dancers in the "snake dance." This dance is done in memory of Inanna, the Sumerian goddess, whose story is filled with death and rebirth. The dance begins by joining hands with other dancers, circling, and chanting. The part that invites and intrigues me is the movement when each dancer stands alone and reaches down with both hands on the left side of the body, stretching low to the earth, then turns in a spiral fashion toward the right, up to the sky. This spiraling, which is done four times—to the North, South, East, and West, is meant to be the movement of a snake shedding its skin. It symbolizes the universal truth of life's transformation: all change involves some skin-shedding. When I participate in the skin-shedding dance, I feel absorbed in the truth of transformation. I see how all-encompassing and demanding it is: the old protective skin falling off so there is room to grow and the vulnerability as new skin develops.

Transformation is a process of death and rebirth. Change is a prerequisite for growth. It involves a "dying" of some sort if new life is going to burst forth. Sometimes I've felt this changing as a radical, painful stripping away, and at other times I've welcomed it like a silent snake slipping out of an old skin that no longer fits. Either way, it has demanded some dying to who I have been and some letting go of what I have known. I now realize that my transformation is an ongoing process. Always there is more skin shedding to do, but in midlife the skins seem to pile up in a hurry on the front doorstep.

So many skins have fallen off of "me" in my midlife journey. My "skins" have included old messages and assumptions about life that developed in my childhood, behaviors that bound me to unhealthy ways of approaching life, religious beliefs that kept my spiritual world too small, and boxed-in views of my self-identity. Skin-shedding has been a time of discovering what keep me from growing.

I have pursued truth, albeit unwillingly at times, and have discovered both treasures and trash in my life. Whenever I have shed any of these skins of mine, I have found freedom and truth. These discoveries have made the transformation process worth the risk and the struggle.

All sorts of fears usually enter into my skin-shedding: fear of the pain that goes with dying, fear of the unknown something that is being birthed, fear of the emotions that might arise, fear of depression, fear of others' criticism or judgments, fear of vulnerability, fear of the length of time it might take for the death/rebirth to occur. These fears can keep me from entering into the transformative process. Kathleen Norris writes: "Fear is not a bad place to start a spiritual journey. If you know what makes you afraid, you can see more clearly that the way out is through fear." When I name my fears, I can usually surrender to the struggle that is happening.

I've had numerous dreams that called me out of my fear and into courage. One in particular had a profound effect on my growth. At a point in midlife when I was facing the option of choosing some new theories and untried behavior, I dreamed that I was in a social situation where there was a large table full of food. This table stretched across the entire room. It held a bounty of colorful, peculiar-looking, unknown foods. I stood among all the strangers who were in the room ignoring me and I wondered what food I might choose at the table that would be "safe." The only thing there that I recognized was egg salad, so I put a large helping of this on my plate and walked away from the table. When I woke up, I laughed. There are few foods that I dislike, but egg salad is one of them. Yet, in my dream, I chose the egg salad, which was a "safe" food because I knew it. How loudly this spoke to my fear of insecurity and of risking some new nourishment for myself. I resolved that day to let go of my "egg salad" approach to life.

The skin-shedding process of transformation in midlife has called me to look at what I believe to be truth, to step into the pain of my disillusionments and fading dreams, to see how my ego attempts to rule me and keep me in bondage so that I am not open to the revelation that my unconscious yearns to share. Skin-shedding has brought me the task of evaluating my persona (the "faces" I show to the world) and discerning which of these, if any, needs to be cast off. Skin-shedding has led me to peer into my Shadow and to discover treasures of my Self as well as those parts that I would rather not own. Letting go of old skins has also drawn me to see my limitations, my weaknesses, and my sin.

In my early thirties, I was overcome with what I considered to be my sinfulness. A big part of this was due to the emphasis in the Roman Catholic Church and in religious life on perfectionism. While I needed to learn and accept the part of me that was capable of sin, I also needed to acknowledge that much of what I thought to be sin was not so at all. This "sin" was actually the pieces of myself I wanted to spurn or reject, those unmanageable things that were a part of being human—unwanted emotions and personality traits. I wanted to "be perfect" but I had to come to terms and be at peace with my clay feet instead:

> Yesterday afternoon as I listened to Handel's music, I imaged myself dancing before you, God. Suddenly I was aware of how poor I am—my clothes were all torn and dirty—but then, I looked into your face and I immediately knew it was okay—that I was totally accepted by you, wonderfully, and then you came and took my hand and we danced together. (Journal)

When I acknowledged and accepted pieces of my Shadow that I had rejected (tenacious, stubborn, strong-willed, tough, determined) I saw that these very things were also some of my treasures. They had helped me to have courage and to survive some difficult life situations. They had also helped me to be steadfast in my love and care. They blessed me with much needed resiliency.

I continued looking for "a giant key" to unlock my inside door, to reveal other hidden treasures, but most of all, to let me into the secret area where I could find the answers to my life's creative tensions. As I did this, I discovered and claimed some of the unwanted parts of my Shadow as well as some of the desirable aspects such as my intuition and instinctual nature, playfulness, joy and childlike wonder.

Acceptance of the golden piece of playfulness took awhile. I was caught up in work and productivity. There is nothing wrong with work and success, but I felt pushed and shoved around by it, so much so that I didn't know how to play anymore. Numerous times I identified with the person in the Christian scriptures who is "possessed" and lives among the tombs. My crazy busyness, with the obsessive pressure of "so much to do," often felt like this insane person.

I wanted some sort of miraculous inner vision like that of the person in the tombs. I wanted a deep seeing that would free me of that tomb-state in me regarding my craziness of work. I started talking to the "voice" in me that always said, "Hurray!" but it took me five years to slow down. During that time, I did a lot of reading and reflection. From this, I realized that I needed to look at the powerful hold that the "negative animus" had on my life. My animus (my inner masculine) had, indeed, tried "to over-run and suppress the feminine principle in me." My negative animus took over in these ways: needing to be right, believing that I had to be rational, logical, and independent, distrusting my intuition, and ignoring my feelings. I had strong opinions and was always into *doing* and frantic busyness. I was organized, well-scheduled, and responsible. I longed for a more contemplative approach to life but I constantly chose *doing* over *being*. Doing was safer and kept me from acknowledging my feelings and my vulnerability.

I learned my busyness from my Western culture, my German heritage, my farmer-father, from the Roman Catholic Church, and from my religious community. They all said basically the same thing: use your gifts, give generously of yourself, work, work, work, don't fail, be successful. I can still hear my father's voice when, as children, we didn't do our chores: "What are you good for?" Again, "If anyone around here wants to eat, they have to work." Again, images helped me to identify both the experience and my feelings. An image of a wild river gave expression to my frustration and stress. The river was wild and strong and I was caught in the current, struggling to hang on. It was a joyless trip full of work, an unending journey that could never find a destination.

Sometimes coming to truth felt like chewing into something hard and tough that had been there for a long time. I was never sure, at first, what it was but it felt somewhat like a new tooth pushing its way to the surface. I could feel it and it was often irritating or painful but I couldn't hurry its growth. I had to wait for it to push its way out.

As much as I wanted truth, I also resisted. When I felt a stretching to new beliefs, I found myself backing off or hoping to ignore the tension. This experience felt "like a rubber band, all stretched out at one moment, ready to break. Then, the next, all shoved together unable to breathe, a back and forth thing, either too taut or else too cramped" (Journal). Always I needed the balance of being compassionate toward myself but also not fleeing from what would bring me necessary growth.

The transformative process of sloughing off the false Self and claiming the true Self has seemed, at times, like a wrestling match or a battle:

> There's a wildness howling outside and a lot of wild things howling inside too. Needing and yearning to be tamed. Something in me wants to keep on running. Something in me wants to be stilled. Part of me feels loved by God. Part of me feels abandoned. (Journal)

The inner battle has been filled with contrasts or "sides": good times and lonely times and times that seemed eternally empty. There were times of tear-full beauty. There were times of tension and stress and times of profound union with God. One day in early April, I saw my midlife battle reflected in rain and snow. It seemed to me that they were arguing, pelting each other with their coldness. Snow threatened to take over the talk but rain had warm air on her side and held her own in the battle. The two, rain and snow, twirled and tumbled, a driving force in each of their voices as they fell to the ground in fury. This was typical of the driving forces within me as I searched for truth and sometimes did not like what I found.

I felt a particular ongoing battle with my ego. I could see how I let my ego push me around, shove me into work, and thrust me into an unhealthy bent toward productivity and intense success-orientation until I felt so pressured I could hardly stand it. Sometimes my true Self strongly confronted me and challenged me about this:

> Do you know what time with me would mean for you? You would feel free. You would discover beauty beyond what you've ever imagined. You would not fret and stew over your own selfish compulsions and needs and wants. You would be a wise woman. Now you are only a carrier of the trinkets of the ego. They melt like sherbet in a summer's sun. Let go before it is too late and you are so ego-absorbed that you do not hear my voice calling you. Stop! You cannot go on this way. You were born to grow deep. You cannot do it, satisfying your ego always. Let go. Risk failure and misunderstanding. Let me be your guide and friend. I love you. (Journal)

This battle with the ego lasted about ten years. It was a constant struggle to let go of some of the security of what I thought I knew for the vulnerability of the unknown.

Some writers use the terms "transformation" and "conversion" interchangeably, both describing the process of growth.

I view conversion as *a piece* of transformation, a process that leads to greater transformation. It has to do with the changing of my heart, befriending what will always be a part of me—my personal limitations and weaknesses—and casting aside what is avoidable: my unhealthy attitudes and behaviors and my choices and decisions for non-good. Countless images related to conversion have spoken to me in my personal journals:

- A huge, hard boulder inside of me, blocking goodness.
- Looking out the window at the brittle, dead branches of winter trees and sensing the brittleness within myself.
- A thorn branch I found in one of my desolate walks when I was working with Shadow material I did not want.
- The discordant cawing of crows that sounded like my false self being judgmental and hateful.
- Ice sliding into a spring river—the hardness in me being willing to soften.
- The walls I put up that kept others out: those who begged my understanding, who needed my forgiveness, who could have grown had I been humble, who would have laughed if I had shared my joy.
- The black, dead trees of a lake that stood in the water, sticking up, poking at me, speaking of the clumps of deadness in my heart.
- Myself as a beggar, poor and empty.
- A rock covering a moist patch of ground, keeping the seeds beneath it from growing.
- A piece of wood in a fast river current being taken for a ride like a small piece of weakness tugged from my heart.
- The weeds in a garden with their deep, tough roots: some could be pulled out, others kept coming back.
- A fresh snowfall contrasted with the bleak grime that I felt inside.

I have also found images of conversion in my dreams. One night I dreamed that I stood by a small pond on a lonely farm. I carefully wrote down all my weaknesses on the many dead leaves that were piled at the water's edge. I tossed them, each leaf, each worded weakness, into the quiet water, but the leaves kept coming back to me. No current or stream would sweep them into an unknown waterway. And so it was with my life. My weaknesses kept returning to haunt me, no matter how often I tossed them away. This was a turning point for me. I had wanted to weed out all of the "bad stuff" from my life. I began accepting the truth that I would always have weaknesses and limitations. I would always have a part of myself that had the potential for all the evil of the world. It was a call to accept myself as I am and to see these parts of myself as my "teachers." It was also a call to accept the flawed condition of others.

Every touch of truth has taken me to where my true Self lives. All of these images and experiences have helped me to continue in the process of transformation and to allow the skins to fall off when the time was ripe. In my twenties I thought I could do little wrong. In my thirties I woke up to all my flaws and was greatly dismayed. In my forties, I began to sort out what I wanted to keep and what I needed to toss away, realizing that some of those flaws would be with me forever. As I move into fifties and beyond, I am growing into the wisdom of accepting myself as I am with my goodness and with my weaknesses, knowing that the process of transformation goes on and on. I can be at home with who I am and be more gentle with others because I have become more gentle with myself.

—*Dear Heart*, 104–13

SEEKING AND FINDING

I search for God,
elusive, hidden God,
I long to dwell
in the heart of Mystery.

I search for my true self
more of who I already am,
knowing there's so much
yet to be discovered.

I search for love,
the unconditional love
that enfolds me
and asks to be shared.

I search for vision
in the shadows of my soul,
impatiently awaiting
the moment of lighting.

I search for a quiet heart
amid life's harried schedule;
my soul cries out,
yearning for solitude.

I search for compassion
in a world gone deaf
to the cries of the hurting,
and the pleas of the powerless.

I search for Home,
always for Home,
unaware, of course,
that I am already there.

*When you search for me, you will find me; when you
search wholeheartedly for me, I shall let you find me.*

—Jeremiah 29:13

Deep within us is a place where we have found God and God
has found us. Once in a great while we come to this place within
us and realize it is the goal of our seeking. It feels like home.
This is a place of safety and security, an ideal home where we
can be ourselves and know we are accepted for who we are. We
have easy access to understanding and acceptance. We may be

challenged to grow here, but always in the context of a deep and strong love.

Thomas Merton writes that when we find our true self we find God, and when we find God we find our true self. Whenever we come to a greater truth about ourselves, we enter this ideal home. Stirrings within us that call us beyond the known, unexpected joys and painful awakenings lead to this home within. We also enter it when a deep contentment and consolation fills our being.

Our hearts and minds are easily distracted by many other things, everyday realities such as work, maintaining a physical home, raising a family, shopping for life's necessities. As much as we yearn to stay closely connected with this inner source we quickly lose our sense of it. Thus, we spend most of our lives seeking what we momentarily find and then lose again.

Most of the time we search without really being aware of what is gnawing at us deep inside. We search for something called happiness. We long for a gift named peace. We search for meaning in our lives, for love, for understanding of ourselves and others, for an acceptance of the ups and downs of the human condition.

Beneath all this longing is the desire for someone or something that feels like home. We are like the young boy who spoke of a visit from "the loneliness birds" as a way to describe his intense inner ache when he would long to be at home with others and to be accepted for who he was. Most of us have "loneliness birds" inside of us at one time or another when we feel this intense desire for something we cannot name but know we need.

We may not be consciously aware of our seeking. We may be living our lives day by day. The wonder is that while this searching goes on within us, there is also One who keeps seeking us out, calling to us, greatly desiring that we find the home within. This One, our inner source whom many call "God," remains a mystery no matter what our image may be. Just when we think we can wrap our arms around God and have God all to ourselves something happens and we find ourselves once again seeking this elusive One. It is the way of the human spirit. It is the way life happens.

I have experienced God seeking me out. I find these moments humbling and deeply cherish them. It happens when something gives me an inner direction that I didn't even know I was looking for—an article or a song, a scripture passage, the words of a friend or a stranger help me form stronger connections with my inner story. It may be an intuition to be among the beauty of the earth which calls to me and gives me clearer vision, or a sense of inner affirmation that was not there before.

One of the most tender moments of God seeking me out happened at the time of my father's death. I had just arrived at a hotel in Honolulu after a very long and tiring flight when I received a message that there was a family emergency. The phone call left me stunned by the news that my dad had died of a heart attack. I rushed back to the airport to catch the first flight home. I was alone as I waited in the long ticket lines. My pain was overwhelming. I could not stop crying. I was overcome with grief and didn't know how I could ever endure the night and day journey back all by myself. In my deep grief I had forgotten how God seeks us out with great love.

I boarded the plane and had just gotten seated when the flight attendant came down the aisle with a tiny Japanese boy about six years old. He looked very frightened as she buckled him into the seat next to mine. He, too, had tears in his eyes. I wiped my own tears and said hello to him. He looked away in fear and shyness. But as the hours slowly went by, this little stranger began to speak with me and to ask me questions.

This small child was a wonderful gift from God. I helped him with his meal. I read stories to him from his little fairy tale book. I listened to his questions and smiled at his wonderings. All the while this child was unknowingly tending to my grieving heart. He kept me from being overcome by my own pain and helped me put my dad's death in momentary perspective. I have often looked back at that sorrowful plane ride and rejoiced at how God's love and compassion sought me in such an unexpected way.

Some of my favorite scripture stories are about people who were sought and found by God. One, a short merchant named Zacchaeus, was anxious to see what kind of man Jesus was and climbed a tree to do so. He only wanted to check out this famous person from a distance. He never expected the consequences. Suddenly Jesus was looking up at him and saying, "Zacchaeus, hurry and come down; for I must stay at your house today." Zacchaeus had been sought and found (Lk 19:1–10, NRSV).

A different kind of seeking occurred with the woman who had suffered from hemorrhaging for twelve years. "She had heard about Jesus, and she came up through the crowd" (Mk 5:27). She sought Jesus, but carefully, because of the cultural taboos regarding a woman in menstruation. She could have been stoned to death for touching someone in public.

Her courageous seeking is rewarded. Power moves through Jesus as she touches the hem of his garment. As she quietly walks away, knowing she has been healed, a wondrous thing happens: Jesus seeks her out in the crowd. He "continued to look all round to see who had done it." He must have had a strong sense of this woman's presence and of the bonding that occurred. When he finds the woman, Jesus affirms her for her great faith (Mk 5:25–34).

Another woman wasn't even seeking Jesus when he came and found her. The Samaritan woman was simply trudging along in her weariness. Her life was a mess. She sought only to get water for another day. Jesus came to the well and led her gently to the home she had not yet found, the goodness of her true self. At first she resisted his seeking. She could not believe that so much love and goodness could be hers, but his loving presence won her over. She would never be the same now that she had been found by him. She immediately ran to seek others and tell them about the powerful thing that had happened to her (Jn 4:1–42).

Many other stories in the Hebrew and Christian scriptures tell of this seeking and finding. Always it is the discovery of a truth already present: the Beloved One is ever near. It is ironic that we search for God when the Divine dwells deep within us, pervading our soul.

The seeking and finding that we do is actually a discovery of a truth already present. When God searches for us, we receive the gift of seeing how God is already with us. It may be just a glimmer but our vision is a bit more clear. Our moments of connection, of finding or being found, convince us more and more of the reality of the home within us.

How do we know when God is seeking us out? Many times God is seeking us out when we sense the following:

- restlessness within or an unnamed loneliness
- a hunger for deep bonding
- questions that keep surfacing
- sudden awareness or clearer vision about life's meaning
- an unexpected sense of deep contentment or peace
- darkness that has the aura of mystery and searching
- a desire for greater truth
- a hopefulness that rises in one's spirit
- a yearning for justice
- an overwhelming awareness of God's mercy
- a bonding with beauty.

How do we know when we are seeking God out? Again it is not always a known or certain thing, but some aspects I have experienced are:

- willingness to sit with the unnamed stirrings within
- the discipline of reflecting, pondering, meditating
- confrontation of fears, anxieties, and concerns
- deliberate decisions to go deeper
- owning and claiming one's inherent goodness
- savoring the beauty of creation
- entering into situations that involve risk and struggle

- actively bonding with a community or others who seek God
- welcoming the goodness in others.

As we continue on the journey of seeking and finding, remember that it is usually a slow process; it takes patience and a strong belief in the power of discovery. We must keep warming the heart with the embers of remembered glimpses or feelings of home. It is also vital to have companions to share the journey with us. We experience great comfort and strength when others seek along with us.

When we discover kinship with another or feel a desire to have some of another person's qualities of goodness, we have a sense of finding our way home. It may feel as though we have known this person for a long time. We feel as though we've found a part of ourselves; to a certain extent, we have.

We can also discover our home when we hear another's story of seeking. We resonate so much with the story that our own seeking is greatly energized. The search seems more real. It seems possible. It's as if another person's story beckons to us to believe that our own home is real. It's like driving down a dark street and coming upon a sturdy house with lights shining behind the windows. We know that even though we have not yet arrived home, we can draw comfort and hope from the sense that some-one else has found a place to belong.

I know a woman who had felt vast emptiness and darkness on her inner journey. She had spoken with me about this hol-lowness many times. Nothing seemed to penetrate the barrier of meaninglessness that she experienced. One day she happened to be in a bookstore and as she leaned over a stack of books she saw a book about darkness. The book seemed to seek her out. She said she felt compelled to buy it. As she read the author's story of struggling with darkness, this woman found a new sense of hope. She had finally found someone who named her

experience for her. She knew she was not alone in her seeking. Another person's search for home gave her a glimpse of
her own.

Sometimes all we have for long stretches of time are glimpses
of home. We have just enough sense of our inner source to keep
us yearning for more. We need to remember that God always
takes the initiative of seeking, placing the desire in our hearts to
be found. Let us keep ourselves available to be found. Let us not
hide out in our fears or in our busyness or our ego-centeredness.
Let us not be so absorbed in our pain or in our anxieties that we
evade the searching love of the One who yearns to help us find
our way home.

—*May I Dance*, 92–100

ONE WHO BRINGS US HOME

You are like those long night trips
When my parents brought me home
After an evening away visiting friends.
I fell fast asleep in the car's backseat
And when we finally made our arrival
One of them carried me quietly to bed.
So it is with You Who Brings Us Home.
When we entrust ourselves to your love,
You carry us quietly in your loving arms,
Bringing us back to where we belong.

Today: I entrust myself to
the *One Who Brings Us Home*.

—*Fragments*, September 23

2

Earth

The world is charged with the grandeur of God.

—*Gerard Manley Hopkins*

Keep close to Nature's heart . . . and break clear away, once in a while, and climb a mountain or spend a week in the woods. Wash your spirit clean.

—*John Muir*

When Joyce Rupp became a Sister she became a little bit like Caine in the TV series Kung Fu: *She walked the earth, fell in love with it, met new people, and helped them.*

Joyce walks at least three miles every day, in every country she has been in, rain or shine, snow or sleet. She has trekked 450 miles across northern Spain on the Camino de Santiago, walked a three-day pilgrimage from Notre Dame in Paris to the cathedral in Chartres, walked a week on the Underground Railway route in Alabama in torrid weather, and has hiked fifteen summers in the Rockies of Colorado. Only icy paths keep her home.

And she always takes time to sit still and hear and see. She is shy but loves to be with people and get to know them.

The following readings illustrate Joyce's communion with Earth and its inhabitants and some of the spiritual lessons learned.

*Of particular interest are two excerpts from an essay she wrote
in the* National Catholic Rural Life Newsletter *in the year 2000,
"Let the Land Teach Us." As a Sister in the early 1980s Joyce
served in five rural parishes in Iowa's Harrison County during a
period of great crisis. She was with many families who lost their
land and knew of farmers who took their lives. This essay on the
plight of rural America is remarkable not only because it was
written by a Sister but for the power of its prose and depth of
spiritual understanding. The farmer's daughter knew what she
was talking about.*

> At its heart, the journey of each life
> is a pilgrimage,
> through unforeseen and sacred places
> that enlarge and enrich the soul.
> —John O'Donohue

LONG AGO I FELL IN LOVE WITH EARTH

*Snow was heavy on the evergreens, but on the leafless
twigs it had been turned to glass. A lovely rosy glow
enveloped the whole landscape but the touch that made
it unusual and breath-taking was that every twig of glass
was turned to amethyst—do you wonder tears formed
in my eyes?*

—*Rachel Carson*

Tears come easily when something of Earth's beauty surprises or
astounds me. The inherent mystery and unspoken magnificence
of the simplest things can move me deeply. It is humbling to
experience Earth's treasures. In being so awed I realize what a
gift it is that I could be privy to such loveliness.

The tears arise because of the intimacy inherent in the experience. At times Earth's beauty unites me with a presence that
is as near as my own soul, yet enormously more expansive. It
is as if, in that experience of recognition, I leave my "self" and

travel into the beauty that is before me. At times like this, Earth draws my being toward the Great Being and invites me into the dynamic dance that is always in cosmic motion.

Long ago I fell in love with Earth and am deeply grateful for all I have come to know and experience of this incredible planet. Earth is a precious part of my life, a wonderful nurturing mother to me, always providing for my needs. Every day she offers me food to eat, air to breathe, and beauty to behold. I recreate in her parks, hike her mountains, and swim in her seas. I find delight in her colors, shapes, and sounds. I receive solace and renewal in her many forms of life. I discover teachings through her creatures and her seasons. No wonder I have a strong and enduring love for the many aspects of this immense and lovely globe of life.

I know this closeness to Earth is not true for all people. Annie Dillard, Earthy mystic, believes this appreciative relationship starts as a young child. This is true and yet it can also be cultivated as an adult. I know a woman who was in her fifties before she fell in love with hills and trees. There are others, though, who seem unable to have an intimate connection with Earth. I once heard someone say, to my great dismay, "Oh, if you've seen one mountain, you've seen them all."

It pains me to think anyone could miss the great diversity and variety that forms our planet. Just think of a few things that Earth is composed of: glaciers, hot springs, waterfalls, tinkling springs; caves, hollows, shady groves, wide forests; turf, sand, loam soil, clay, and stone; peninsulas, fjords, islands, flats, swamps; wilderness, desert, mesas, orchards, farmlands, bogs, paddies; savannas, meadows, plateaus, and plains; mountains, bluffs, valleys, ledges, cliffs, crevices; glens, harbors, lakes, rivers, creeks, and vast seas. To say nothing at all of the immense number and types of creatures that live on and within the treasure of this planet. Add to all of this the diverse textures plus colors of every shade and hue within the immense composition of Earth. To contemplate this for any length of time simply boggles my mind and races my heart.

There are many different kinds of places on our planet. These aspects of Earth influence and help to shape our psyches. We feel more at home in one place of Earth than another. I recall author Sam Keen saying, when he spoke in a Midwest city, that he could hardly stand all the green there. It was too much for him. He lived in the dried, brown land of western ranch country and felt alien in the rich, moist green farmland. My friend, Aileen, grew up on an island and took a ferry to school every day in New Zealand. She said she did not understand, at first, why she felt so terribly depressed when she went to live inland where the sea could not be seen. Another friend has never gotten over her homesickness for the white paper birch trees and the great waves of Lake Superior in northern Michigan. Yet another relishes the energy and vibrancy of a large city. Some enjoy the endless sun of tropics or the frozen land of the north, while others are at peace among rainy days and fog.

I have lived most of my life on this planet in the Midwest where there are four very strong, distinct seasons. They have taught me many valuable lessons of life and I would miss them greatly if I lived elsewhere. Earth has brought me strength and courage through winter's endurance, hope and enthusiasm as spring awakens the land, gratitude and contentment in summer's fruitfulness, and wisdom from autumn's ability to let go and yield to dormancy and death.

My relationship with Earth continues to grow and strengthen as I make a deliberate effort to spend time with the many facets of our planet. Each day I go for a walk no matter what the weather and I eat outdoors as much as possible. In the wintertime houseplants keep me close to nature, as well as fresh flowers in a vase. When I travel I make a deliberate effort to notice the landscape wherever I may be. I pay attention to Earth through the vegetables, fruits, and other food items as I prepare a meal and through the water in a steaming bath or shower.

There have been situations where there was little nature to behold for a good portion of my day (a windowless office or conference hall, a stuffy meeting room . . .) but even then I have been able to connect with Earth by noticing the food I eat and the water I drink. I've also used photos of nature on the covers of my journals and for bookmarks so that I am easily reminded of Earth's goodness.

As I have aged, it occurs to me that one of the most difficult things about dying will be leaving this amazing planet. The unknowns of the "beyond" do not bother me much. It's the "giving up" of this life so intertwined with the beauty and goodness of Earth that causes me concern. She claimed my heart long ago and I ache, even now, at the thought of never roaming her woods, walking by her rivers, touching her green, listening to the birds, feeling the sting of her sharp wind on my cheeks, looking at her soft, silent snowfalls, or catching a glimpse of deer or foxes at play. What joy can be beyond this side of life to equal what I have known here in beauty? I simply must trust—like the unborn babe who swims in the beauty of life within the womb—that beyond what I know here there is something else equally as beautiful and it will claim my heart as fully.

—*Cosmic Dance*, 59–61

NATURE HAS BEEN A WONDERFUL SOURCE OF HEALING FOR ME

Nature has been a wonderful source of healing for me. It is often through nature that I find the insight and the courage to let go, to surrender, to move on. The following are some insights that have blessed me with moments of healing when I was in desperate need of them:

Fireflies in the dusk: I was walking out a great loneliness in my life one night. As I moved along the wooded path, I saw a bright light in the distance. I quietly drew closer and saw that it was only one tiny firefly. It was just a small fragile frame that was giving forth such brightness! The lone firefly then joined the dance of a hundred fireflies as I walked in the late dusk. All across the vast meadow, far into the woods, their little lights danced and brought me a sense of bondedness. They were like a silent symphony, a gift to my lonely spirit. Like Christmas tree lights without the strings to mar their freedom, the fireflies held vigil with me. They danced for the earth, giving light to its darkness, and I thought they danced for me, a pure and simple gift of beauty in the night.

In our darkest hour, it is often the smallest spark that brings us the gift of light, be it ever so frail a flicker. It is the moment of simple grace in a softly spoken word, a letter from a friend, an unexpected phone call, a warm touch from a loved one, or even a glance at the earth in its moment of hope. God has blessed our spirits with his own fireflies. They are small and fragile, but they fly in our dark woods and their little beaming lights seem brilliant in our need.

Trees: Probably the most healing gifts of nature for me have been trees. I am rarely with trees for very long without a sense of blessedness or the truth of goodbye resting in my spirit. I once spent an autumn weekend with an oak tree. I watched the old oak with its wide-reaching arms give away his summer celebration. All night and all day the dead, brown leaves fluttered and flapped across the porch to the ground. Each little rap of wind tugged at the branches and lifted off another leaf. It seemed to me that the old oak tree stood ready and surrendered to the autumn event. I felt like an intruder on his farewell, seeing the wide open, stretched out limbs, the quiet, peaceful stance of his letting go. On that particular weekend, the wisdom of surrender was rooted much more deeply in me.

The Flight of Geese: In the country place where I used to live, I would often be awakened in the night by the sound of geese going south for the winter. It was a welcome sound that always left my heart feeling a bit sad and a bit glad. Geese speak to the part of me that knows transition and change are necessary, that leaving secure situations is an essential part of growth. When I hear flocks of geese call and see their patterned flight, they encourage me to allow myself to stretch and to grow. There is also a part of me that fills with nostalgia. My spirit cries out to them: "Friends!" The flight of geese helps me to recall all the blessings that change and transition have meant for my own growth and all the special people who have walked through my heart because I have moved on. The migration of geese, and all birds, deepens the belief in me to keep traveling the inner roads when I would rather not go.

Frost: One winter morning I awoke to see magnificent lines of frost stretching across my window panes. They seemed to rise with the sunshine and the bitter cold outside. They looked like little miracles that had been formed in the dark of night. I watched them in sheer amazement and marveled that such beautiful forms could be born during such a winter-cold night. Yet, as I pondered them I thought of how life is so like that. We live our long, worn days in the shadows, in what often feels like barren, cold winter, so unaware of the miracles that are being created in our spirits. It takes the sudden daylight, some unexpected surprise of life, to cause our gaze to look upon a simple, stunning growth that has happened quietly inside us. Like frost designs on a winter window, they bring us beyond life's fragmentation and remind us that we are not nearly as lost as we thought we were, that all the time we thought we were dead inside, beautiful things were being born in us. —*Goodbyes,* 85–87

A CREED FOR THE SOWING OF SEEDS

A man throws seed on the land. Night and day, while he sleeps, when he is awake, the seed is sprouting and growing; how, he does not know.

—*Mark 4:26–28*

I believe that this is one of the earth's finest moments, that the sun lifting yellows and greens into life of tiny poplar leaves is much like God's own Spirit of love lifting the life into me.

I believe that the Word of God has many times been planted in my life, often because of another who received the seed in ready soil, brought forth a harvest, and shared that goodness with me.

I believe that the call to be a sower of the Word is a privilege and a blessing, that no one can ever earn the right or claim the duty, that it is a gift freely given and a ministry to be constantly celebrated in gratitude.

I believe that great things can come forth from even the tiniest seed planted in love and cared for tenderly in the heart of another.

I believe that usually only God knows what sprouting and greening will come from the Word planted through my ministry. I am content in knowing that I have tried, with the Sower's grace, to seed that Word in faith and with joy.

I believe that even the most insignificant aspects of life can be the seed of God's gifting, that deeper faith can root and mature in very ordinary soil.

I believe that some dying of seed has to take place before it can give itself over to life, that every heart has its germination time, its dark moment, before the future hallowedness of harvest comes.

I believe that it takes much patience to sow a seed, to freely give it away to the heart of earth, to allow it to take root and to grow in its own good time.

I believe that my life will always know its season of hope, that I will find flowers after every finality of ice and snow, that I will find green, growing things after every harsh, barren reign of winter's rage.

and most of all . . .

I believe in the Sower of all seeds, in the God of Springtime, in the Giver of all good and growing things, my Lord and my God!

—*Fresh Bread*, 73–74

"SEED-SONG"

I am the seed
so small, so dry,
lifted in the hand
of the silent Sower.

into the earth
I fearfully fall,
darkness covers me,
silence surrounds me.

the terror of my heart
is the only sound
to keep me company.

all that is me
huddles together
trying desperately
not to surrender
any part of self.

"why was I planted?"
I cry out.
"why am I here?"
I entreat.
"take me out into light;
I cannot bear
this deathly dark."

I weary. I weaken.
the days become long.
I can no longer fight.
I surrender
in this lonely place
of waiting.

quietly I sense
a penetrating warmth;
it surrounds me;
it fills me
and blesses my pain.

in a moment
of peacefulness
I forget my fear.

I let go of my self
and suddenly
the husk that holds me
weakens and breaks.

"No!" I scream.
I am losing my self,
but it is too late.
the husk is cracked;
I cannot be contained.

it is then
that I sense a power
deep inside of me,
encouraging me:
"let go. let go. let go."

it is an energy
that pushes the husk
until it falls away.

as it slips aside
my eyes behold color.
ah! can it be?
a tiny glimpse of green!

"how could that be?"
I marvel,
"there was never green
in the heart of me."

yet, it is there;
each day
it slowly stretches upwards
to where the warm seems to be.

I become less of a seed.
I am losing my self
but the pain I once knew
is lost in surprise;
something wonderful
is greening and growing
deep within my heart.

days go quickly now.
I become one
with the small stem of life.

oh! the glorious moment
when, ah, breath of Spring
fast fills my face.
I move through the hard earth
and taste the world which awaits my arrival.

from within my tender shoot
comes a soft sound.
I listen. I hear.
it is a song to the Sower:

O Sower of seeds,
did you always see
this gift of green

that was hiding in me?

O Sower of seeds,
how came you to prize
the beauty within
that I hid from my eyes?

O Sower of seeds,
the husk has been broken;
all praise to you
for helping me open.

Accept now my praise,
my thankfulness, too,
for the seed you have sown
and the gift that you grew.

May you lead me to others
who await your good word,
so the seeds within them
can awake and be heard.

amen! alleluia!

—*Fresh Bread*, 66

A THOUSAND ROOTS

the poet Rilke knew
where to find hope
and why
God is dark, he said,
and like a wondrous web,
a thousand roots
with their hungry mouths
silently sipping
someday I'd like to slip
my head beneath the cover

of earth,
not the six-foot-deep type,
only far enough to see
to let my eyes behold those
sipping, slurping roots,
the tiny feathered ones,
the thick grandfathers,
the long maiden tendrils,
and the bulbous pregnant ones
to listen as they imbibe
delicious moisture
held inside that darkened space
I'd like to take a ride
through the hopeful web,
follow the fresh drink
still moist on the root's mouth,
travel up the green stem,
and hear the sigh of joy
in the fluttering, receptive leaves
—*Cosmic Dance*, 117

A KERNEL OF CORN AND A LITTLE TEAPOT

There is no end to what could be written about prayer, but everything can be succinctly summed up in a poem by Rabindranath Tagore and a story by Dr. Rachel Naomi Remen.

In Tagore's striking poem, a beggar stands waiting for alms. Along comes the Holy One disguised as a person of royalty dressed in rich robes and riding a fine horse. This regal dignitary stops in front of the beggar whose heart leaps with joy in anticipation of a big contribution. To the beggar's great dismay, instead of giving something, the bejeweled personage asks the beggar: "And what do you have to give me?" The disappointed beggar is put off by this unseemly request. He reaches into his tattered sack of belongings and pulls out one kernel of corn which he gives to the dignitary. At the end of the day, this same royal figure returns, comes to where the beggar is sitting, leans over, and places one kernel of gold in the beggar's outstretched hand. As the person of royalty rides away, the beggar weeps with regret, saying, "How I wished I had the heart to give You my all."

In my own life, I am often the beggar reaching in for the one kernel of corn, but once in a while, my heart enlarges enough to present my entire life to the Beloved. In spite of the countless times I have held back and given much less than was asked from my love, I find a long list of gifts spilling over from my journey of prayer. Thanks to God's generosity I have received much more than one little kernel of gold. These blessings include: a certain serenity amid life's continuous ups and downs, direction and guidance, perspective on life and fuller meaning, energizing encouragement and hope, an unmasking of my illusions, awareness of inner goodness and challenges to share the best of who I am, recognition of life as a daily gift, and a deep sense of kinship with all that exists.

> *Life is everywhere, hidden in the most ordinary and unlikely places. . . . All it needs is your faithfulness.*

And now for the story. In *My Grandfather's Blessings*, Rachel Naomi Remen tells of an endearing grandfather who brought presents when he came to visit her. One day, when she was four years old and living on the sixth floor of an apartment building in New York City, he came with a little paper cup filled with dirt. They went into the nursery together where he found a teapot from her dollhouse set. Her grandfather filled the teapot with water and showed her how to put a few drops of water in the cup, saying: "If you promise to put some water in it every day, you may see something happen." She promised her grandfather she would do this, and then he placed the cup of dirt on the windowsill.

At first, the little girl was interested in seeing what might happen, but as the days went by and nothing changed in the cup of dirt, she found it harder and harder to put water in it. After a week she asked her grandfather if it was time to stop. He told her "no" and added reassuringly, "Keep watering it every day."

The second week was even more difficult for the little girl to put water in the cup, and she started to resent it. She even tried to return the cup to her grandfather. He simply smiled and said, "Every day, every day." By the third week, she sometimes forgot and would have to get out of bed at night to do the watering, but she never missed a single day. Each time she told her grandfather that she wanted to stop, he smiled lovingly and encouraged her with the same words, "Every day."

One morning when she went to put water in the cup, she was astonished to see two little green leaves above the dirt. Each day the leaves grew bigger. She could not wait to tell her grandfather about the wondrous thing that had happened. When he came to visit, he shared her joy at the green leaves and explained to her, "Life is everywhere, hidden in the most ordinary and unlikely places." She was delighted and asked him, "And all it needs is water?" Gently, her grandfather touched her on the top of her head and said, "No, all it needs is your faithfulness." Like this young child who watered the seemingly dead soil in the little cup, we must be willing to faithfully tend our God-relationship each day so it can grow. There will be times when we, too, forget to do the watering, times when we may even resist or resent the practice of prayer, times when we doubt the worth of it, but we keep on "watering," anyhow. As we do so, we renew our trust that little leaves of spiritual growth are sprouting from our daily communication with the beloved companion of our soul.

Like the beggar by the roadside, God requests our generous love. Like the child watering the seeds, God asks our faithfulness. Bring these two gifts to prayer every day and God will do the rest. —*Prayer*, 121–24

TREES TEACH ME

Whenever I spend time with a tree there's always a teaching to help me with whatever is calling me to grow. Sometimes there is nothing in particular stirring in my life, but being with a tree will release a thought in me that serves me well at a future time.

I lean against, lie down under, and stand by trees. I ponder them from my office window and hold hands with them when I pause to touch their branches in the park. My life would be bereft if I did not have a tree or two to keep me company and to teach me things I need to know.

I've learned how to not be broken from life's unwanted things by watching a willow in the wild wind tossing and bending rather than pushing back against the storm. It's taught me that I can't always have everything go my way. Sometimes I need to bend a bit.

Paper birches have reminded me to surrender as their bark peeled off to aid the growth. The ponderosa pines of Colorado have urged me to be resilient as they stood sturdily through the turbulent mountain seasons. Enduring cottonwoods, with their many fibrous roots, have counseled me to sink strong webbing roots of love and faith so I will still be nourished in dry times when I question most everyone and everything.

Old dead trees in the moist woods persuaded me that life can come through death as their decaying bodies nurture soil and seeds. The sycamore's round terminal buds on leafless branches showed me how to wait patiently through the dormant times of my inner winters when all seemed unable and unworthy of growth.

Trees have taught me about hospitality as I've seen them housing animals and birds. The live oaks of Louisiana prompted me to be compassionate as they shaded and protected me with their wide reaching arms. I've learned about unity and community from clumps of aspen groves and poplar shoots that nurture one another.

Fruit and nut trees of all types and tastes have influenced me to give away freely of my work and talents as I saw their bounty harvested for market. The thorns of the honey locust warned me of the price to be paid for the sweet pulp within its twisting pods, not unlike the challenge in the price I once paid amid the thorns of a challenging, yet successful job.

A new green shoot growing from a maple stump assured me that new life can come despite my woundedness, and the mighty redwoods have advised me that aging can be a graceful process with an inherent dignity.

On and on the teachings go. They never end. Not as long as I listen to the trees. —*Cosmic Dance*, 67

THE RESILIENT SPIRIT

We are afflicted in every way, but not crushed;
perplexed, but not driven to despair;
persecuted, but not forsaken;
struck down, but not destroyed . . .
—*2 Cor. 4:8–9*

The sharp delineation of seasonal changes in the Midwest helps me believe in the resiliency of the human spirit. When I walk through the woods amid the stark, barren branches in late autumn or drive along seemingly dead, brown fields stripped of grain, I know that a vibrant green springtime will follow. The barrenness of the land with its inherent promise of new life assures me that I, too, can endure through a silent, empty season, that I, too, have a suppleness to my spirit which will help me bounce back after being flattened by the unwanted and inevitable struggles of life.

Resiliency is rooted in the human heart. It is an essential catalyst for moving through painful and devastating experiences. Resiliency is about being down and out and springing back, being persistent in the face of defeat. It is solidarity with others that strengthens the soul. It is hope that holds on in spite of overwhelming loss. It is unrelenting faith in a loving divinity whose abiding presence provides strength through every season.

I thought a lot about resiliency a few years ago when I went to visit my aunt in California. That year the gardeners had pruned her lemon tree. On previous visits the tree was burgeoning with delicious fruit, branches so weighted they hung all the way to the ground. This particular year, however, the tree was pruned beyond recognition. Almost all the smaller branches were gone, leaving gray blunt stumps, nary a leaf anywhere. I could not imagine that tree ever producing lovely lemons again, but to my great surprise and joy, the lemon tree was green and full of fruit two years later when I returned.

How much we are like that harshly pruned lemon tree when, at the time of a devastating situation, we feel demolished with unspeakable pain. We can't imagine ever feeling good again. So much seems at an end—our joy, our contentment, our peace of mind. We forget in those horrible times, or perhaps have never understood until then, that we are also capable of immense resilience. We can only think of how much distress and hurt we are experiencing.

It is then that the courageous ability to "bounce back" rises up in us, urging us to stand strong. Something abiding and enduring in us stirs and calls: "You can make it through this even though you feel overcome and defeated." Long ago this resiliency was seeded in our soul. It will enable us to bounce back from what threatens to destroy us. It will help us rise up from whatever knocks us down.   —*Cosmic Dance*, 118

LOST IN THE FOG

Quiet Mystery,
today the earth wears mufflers on her ears.
Heavy wet clouds disguise the silent land.
The city is a giant mound of bleary white
with dense fog permeating everything.
Even the sparrow's song sounds thick.
In the concealing mist of morning,
street lights blur with masked revelation,
and walkers are lost in a veil of obscurity.

Secret One of my Soul,
portions of the land within me are dimly lit,
answers to my daily struggles are hazy,

and direction for my future lies hidden.
Often I lose my way as I meander in this inner fog,
struggling to find the path of some deeper peace.

As I reach out in this dim state of my inner domain,
I cry out for you and find you there,
safely leading me amid the mystery.
Quiet me, as fog quiets the external world,
so that I can listen more intently to you.
Draw me further into surrender.
Rest me in your comforting stillness,
and let me be content with what is unclear.

*"I came forth from the mouth of the Most
High, and covered the earth like a mist."*
Ecclesiasticus 24:3
—*Sophia, 64–65*

CHANGING THE LANDSCAPE

It doesn't take much
to change the grey drabness
of a bleak winter day,

just an inch or two of snow
soft upon the lawn and roof.

It doesn't take much
to change the stony landscape
of a rankled heart,

just a word or two of kindness
soft upon the discontent.

It doesn't take much
to change the angry mind
of a quickened hurt,

just an offering of forgiveness
soft upon the injury.

—*My Soul*, 116

WHAT HAVE YOU DONE TO ME?

*From day to night
you bring me to an end.*

—*Isaih 38:13b*

I am the spawning salmon
too weak to swim upstream
I am the sickened song bird
dying from pesticides
I am the unprotected top soil
ripped away by swirling rains
I am the great rivers and lakes
invaded by murky garbage
I am homeless creatures
searching for a lost habitat
I am the emptied rain forest
weeping from being raped
I am the gentle dolphin
tangled in gluttonous fishing nets
I am the graceful antelope
hit by the speeding vehicle
I am all species of plant and creature
threatened, poisoned, destroyed
I am Earth, your nurturing Mother,
wounded and in sore distress
Who will hear my cry?
Who will bear my sorrow?
Who will come to my aid?
Who will free me from my pain?

* * *

> *The difficulty is that. . . we began to think of the universe*
> *as a collection of objects rather than as a communion of*
> *subjects.*   —*Thomas Berry*

As we get to know the sea, mountains, people, creatures, and other inhabitants of Earth, we learn their stories, see where they have been weakened by illness and accidents, discover the pains they have endured in the storms and struggles of life and unexpected events. We learn that death is inevitable, no matter how closely and carefully people and nature are guarded and tended. Natural disasters such as earthquakes, tornadoes, and hurricanes occur because of climatic and seasonal changes. Animals and plants feed on one another in order to live. Everything ages and weakens. Life and death follow one another in a natural cycle and from this cycle new life is eventually birthed.

However, a tremendous amount of pain and destruction is cruel and often preventable. Deaths, meaningless deaths, unwarranted deaths, careless deaths and deliberately callous deaths— they happen all the time. Humans do this to one another and they do this to their environment as well. Soil is washed away due to careless farming practices. Fish die because large factories pollute their waters with refuse. Birds and sea creatures struggle helplessly in huge spills of oil tankers. Limbs of orphaned children are blown to bits by land mines. Humans are lined up and murdered, their bodies thrown into mass graves. The priceless life of many is cut short, all because of attitudes and actions that hasten death and cause needless, excruciating suffering.

Humans have long thought of themselves as superior to the rest of creation and this thinking has promulgated a false sense of authority and dominance, creating the illusion that humans are "better than" and "apart from," rather than intimately connected with the rest of life. Rachel Carson, who first awakened society to the harm that humans were wreaking upon the land through pesticides, wrote: "The control of nature is a phrase conceived in arrogance born out of the Neanderthal age. . . when it was supposed that nature exists for the convenience of man."

Thomas Berry observed that many humans see the world as a collection of things rather than as sacred sources of existence, as individual objects rather than as a part of one great organism in which the experience of each affects the life of all. Humans have become used to taking what they want from Earth without considering the consequences. Much of the unnecessary planetary pain today is caused by humans seeking their own convenience and comfort at the expense of Earth. "Forget the trees, air, water, soil, and creatures," human actions seem to say, "just let us have more shopping malls, larger houses, numerous electrical gadgets, wider highways, water fountains in desert cities . . ."

Something that has helped me in changing my own "dominance attitude" was learning how to "think like a mountain." With this approach, I discovered a way to enter into the life and death of nature by trying to "get inside" what nature was experiencing. I did this by pausing and being present, thinking what it must be like to be a tree enduring many seasons and then quickly cut down, to be the sea with tons of garbage continually shoved into it, to be a mountain when the ancient stones and soil are roughly cut aside to form a road, to be an elk hunted and killed, to be a sea otter whose family faces extinction. When I began to think in this way, I discovered a creation composed not of "things," or "objects," but of sacred companions with as much a right to live and exist as I have.

Because of my changed consciousness, I had a whole different awareness when I read about the grizzly bear's struggle for survival and learned that these great bears have seen their habitat shrink to less than one percent of their former range. I could imagine their loss and hunger as they searched to find a home and enough food for survival. I thought: "It's like if I had been living in a huge estate and now had to live in a closet."

Likewise, I understood the anguish in the voice of a farmer in Wales as she described her sorrow in having her whole herd of cows, three generations of Herefords, shot and killed at the time of the foot and mouth epidemic. With tears streaming down her cheeks she said she knew each of the cows by name and that even if she was blindfolded she would know them by touching their udders from her years of milking them. She knew they had to be killed because they were dying, the skin on their tongues and udders was falling off from the disease.

I understood her grief as well as the suffering of her cows because each part of Earth pains in its own way. All of life is sacred and deserves to be treated with dignity and respect. When creatures and plants generously give their lives so that others might live, those who receive life from them need to do so with awareness and gratitude, remembering the sacrifice that has been made for them.

The pain of Earth and the destructive tendencies of humans are many and will not be easily solved. There are no quick solutions to the problems that exist. For example, how can we make a choice between large river dams that supply vast amounts of electricity and needed irrigation, and the destruction of habitat for millions of fish and other creatures that these dams create? How can we protect the Arctic coastal plains of Alaska, still untamed and rich with herds of caribou, wolves, bears, birds and other wildlife, and also find a way to meet the need of fuel consumers by drilling intrusive oil wells in that area? Creative solutions to the many environmental dilemmas must be sought with unselfish compromise, with an attitude of what is best for ALL involved, always with an awareness of the oneness of life that we share.

We cannot go on as before, none of us. Each action we take has an influence on the rest of life on the planet. Nothing we do remains isolated. Each influences the other. It is a tremendous gift and also, an enormous challenge. As long as Earth remains an "it," a "thing," rather than a living, vibrant reservoir of life, humans will continue to use and abuse her. We need a loving relationship with this generous, vulnerable planet on which we live. Only then will we allow her songs of rich abundance to dance in the rhythms of our lives, only then will we respond with reverent care and live with daily gratitude.

—Cosmic Dance, 97–100

Here are excerpts from the cri de coeur *of a farmer's daughter and Servite Sister that astonished readers of the* National Catholic Rural Life *newsletter in 2000. It not only reveals Joyce's knowledge and understanding of an American crisis but her uncompromising compassion and spiritual take on things: "Every time we come through a winter of our spirit, there's a gift for us."*

LET THE LAND TEACH US

When I speak at conferences, I often ask to be introduced as a farmer's daughter because the experience of growing up on a farm and working the land has greatly influenced both my spirituality and my writing. I have learned much from the land and have been inspired and challenged by what it has taught me. My mother lived in a small town in northwest Iowa and hoped she would marry a farmer so she could live on the land. She often told me stories of her childhood, especially about happy vacations on her grandparents' farm. The land drew her to something deep and strong. I feel these same strong roots in me. My parents loved our farm and took good care of it. That appreciation easily slipped into my heart.

In the early 1980s, I was working in five rural parishes in Iowa's Harrison County. We were going through a farm crisis at that time and I was part of a group who created a program called SPARK, to tend the spiritual and psychological needs of farmers and to encourage them to have hope. I sense that the situation has come full circle, except that what we're currently experiencing in the farm crisis is even more painful and difficult than it was in the eighties. I thought it was very bad then as I went to farm sales and rallies and listened to people's struggles and concerns. During that time I learned about the inherent pain that farming people experienced as they said farewell to their land and to a way of life that had been a source of strength and meaning for them.

The current situation of rural America includes grim prices for products, weather disasters, genetic modification challenges, inadequate farm bills, destruction of soil, pollution of water, and the powerful momentum of consolidation and depopulation that threatens to annihilate a valuable way of life. Amid the luxury of financial growth for much of the United States, it is one of the worst economic times for farmers in this same nation. All of this is readily apparent for those who are in touch with the issues of rural America.

A poem by David Whyte, titled "An Old Interior Angel," speaks to me about rural America's situation and the hope I hold for those struggling in farming. In this poem Whyte describes how he was hiking in Tibet and decided to separate from his party in order to hike by himself for a while. He planned to walk for three days to a certain bridge where he would rejoin his group. In order to do this he would have to cross that bridge and meet them on the other side of it.

All went well until he got to the bridge which hung over a 400 foot chasm. It was then that he saw its condition: all of the top cables of the swinging bridge were broken, as well as many of its wooden planks. Whyte couldn't imagine crossing that bridge. As he sat down near it he felt discouraged and disheartened, deciding he would have to walk back to where he had started.

Just then an old Tibetan woman came shuffling along carrying a basket, gathering dung for fuel. She walked right past him, her eyes on the ground, giving Whyte the "Namaste" Indian greeting as she passed by. (Meaning "I greet the God in you.") Then she walked straight ahead, onto and across the broken bridge without even taking a pause. At that moment something stirred in David Whyte. Seeing this old woman do the seemingly impossible helped him realize that he, too, could cross the bridge. He concludes his poem by calling this woman "an old interior angel," someone who gives him the courage to take action and follow her across the dangerous bridge.

I see the broken bridge as a metaphor for the current barriers rural America faces right now. David Whyte, fearfully sitting at that rickety, scary bridge, is anyone who faces great difficulty and fear. When we get to that bridge we hesitate, doubt, question,—wondering if we can make it to the other side. We've never crossed a bridge so dilapidated before. It looks dangerous and risky to do so. Facing this bridge causes doubts and raises a lot of questions: "Why did I come this way? Why didn't anyone fix that bridge? How am I supposed to get any further? Will I make it if I try to cross over? Do I have to go back instead of forward?" These questions underlie rural America's questions: "Did I make the wrong choice? Can I farm in the future? Will the family farm survive? Who will fix the farm bill? How can I get to the other side of this perilous time? What will I do with the plummeting prices and the problems associated with genetic engineering? Will consolidation destroy rural America's land and way of life?"

When we're in a difficult place, we can get stuck, too paralyzed to move on due to concern for what might happen to us. We can lose hope, believing the only thing for us is to go back into what we know instead of moving creatively into the future. Whyte chose his journey but he did not choose the broken-down bridge, just as those who choose to work the land do not choose all the difficult things that happen in the process of farming.

Does rural America have an "old interior angel?" Yes, I believe it does. It is the land itself. The land can teach us about our inner resiliency and about the process of growth. The land holds many messages about transformation, the movement from death to life. The land can show us how to be open and to trust that we will find creative solutions. It can help us grow through what seems to be impossible obstacles. The land can help us find meaning amid apparently meaningless situations fraught with frustration and pain. The language and the experience of the land can be a source of both spiritual and psychological support. It can teach us how to grieve and how to heal. The land is a sentinel of promise, inviting us to see beyond where we now are and encouraging us to believe that new life will come forth in spite of current struggles.

How can the land do this? By doing what it has always done so well: entering into and giving itself to the process of Earth's four seasons of spring, summer, autumn and winter. The land teaches by showing us that each season is part of the pattern of transformation. It begins with new life and eventually comes through death back to new life again. This transformational cycle of the land is similar to that in scripture. It is the Exodus story with its journey from Egypt (autumn), through the wilderness (winter), into the Promised Land (spring) which finally brings prosperity (summer). This same cycle is in the Christian journey with the birth of Jesus (spring), his public ministry (summer), crucifixion and death (autumn), and three days in the tomb (winter) before being raised from the dead and a new season of spring (Easter) begins.

The land encourages us by its phenomenal resiliency, surviving such challenges as devastating winds, powerful blizzards, months of drought, cruel hailstorms, destructive tornadoes and hurricanes, fierce fires and rampaging floods. The land also teaches by its process of planting and growing. Every farmer knows that a seed must fall into the ground and die before it becomes a new, green shoot. How much easier it is to believe this about a seed than it is to believe it about one's own life, however.

When I look at the four seasons I see our inner human experience as a parallel. In springtime there's vibrancy, life and vitality. Then comes the productive and fruitful summer. Following this is autumn when that which has ripened is taken away and the land begins to shut down. (I've often wondered what it is like for the land when those big combines come through the fields to strip it of everything it has worked so hard to produce.) Finally, in this seasonal cycle there is winter, a time of seeming death in which the land lies fallow. This season is a non-productive, waiting time when the land is re-energizing and renewing itself. The winter land tells us that non-productivity and emptiness are an essential element before new growth and fruitfulness can happen. Yet it is this empty, dark season that most of us find difficult to accept as part of our own transformation cycle.

I believe that the spirit of rural America is in its winter season now. It is a time of dark loss, of empty promises, of barren financial gains, and fallow hope. At a farm rally in August of 1999, Senator Wellstone from Minnesota described rural America as: "a lot of people near the edge that are ready to go under—broken dreams, broken lives, broken families." This is an apt description of winter at it harshest. No wonder this season is one that is fought and avoided even though it is vital for the transformation process.

What can rural America do during this tough time? Before turning toward hope and a new season of spring, its wintered spirit of discouragement and loss must be acknowledged. Many of those who work on the land and love it are now facing unwanted changes and these changes must be recognized for what they are: an experience of loss that has within it a kind of "dying" or diminishment. What makes this loss more intense is that most of America is either not aware of this situation or does not care. With rural America's loss comes grief at what is being taken away without consent. (The word grief is taken from a Latin word gravare which means "to burden or press heavily upon," while bereaved means "to be robbed.")

This loss has many layers to it—it's not just loss of the land. There's loss of an identity. Many people do not continue to farm, finding work in town or in the city. In no longer claiming identity as a farmer there is then the question of "how do I name myself and describe myself?" This loss also involves letting go of a lifestyle and a heritage. There is no more direct contact through working with the land so there is loss of satisfaction as well as the loss of a dream. ("I thought we'd always have this farm"). Sometimes there is also the loss of a relationship. Division and divorce are more likely when couples are going through a time of financial crisis.

Grief, with its bewildering and unwanted feelings, needs to be tended. Those who grieve cannot isolate themselves from others, although this is often the inclination of the independent farmer. There's a need for support when one is grieving; it is not healthy to "go it alone." In the last farm crisis I remember despairing farmers who took their lives and others who went into severe clinical depression. It was very difficult to get those who were hurting to talk about their inner experience. We need to assure those who are experiencing hurt that they have our support and care. Even though we may not live on a farm, we can be closely united with the farming community and grieve with them when we sense the great loss that is presently sweeping rural America.

Grieving farmers need the strength of community. Again, we can learn from the land. How is the land community-oriented? Think of a crop in the field. If you have just one stalk of corn or one sheaf of wheat when a windstorm comes along or long days of hot sun beat down, it is not going to stand up straight for very long or find much moisture, but if you have a whole lot of cornstalks or sheaves of wheat around it, that lone stalk or sheaf is much stronger, more protected, and will contain moisture longer.

How do we find meaning in the midst of this crisis? I think it is very difficult but not impossible. One thing is certain—we need to keep hope alive. Author Anne Lamott describes hope in this way: "Hope begins in the dark, the stubborn hope that if you just show up and do what is right, the dawn will come. You wait, you watch, and you work, and you don't give up." Hope begins in the *dark*. If we can approach the current farm crisis with a belief that there will be another springtime, we will not give up. Rather, we will trust that this troubled time can lead to something new. Indeed, we would believe that this difficult moment in rural America's history is essential for something creative and vibrant to evolve.

—*NCRL*, February 23

WHY DIDN'T YOU TELL ME
THIS LLAMA WAS BORN?

Sometimes our boxed-in views and ideas crowd out creativity and new life because we cling too tightly to our past experience and certainties. When I was in living in a Benedictine retreat center in Colorado, the Sisters there had started raising llamas on their farm. Mama llama was pregnant. I had never seen a pregnant llama before so I couldn't wait for this llama to have her baby. I presumed the process would be like every other farm animal I had known. Everyday I'd look and wonder if the baby had come yet. One day I was walking across the yard as I went over to the abbey and, lo, there I saw the baby llama! I was disappointed that I had missed the birth, thinking "why didn't anybody tell me this llama was born?" I looked at the baby in wonder. She was just beautiful, standing there in her dry, pure white coat.

I walked to the abbey and said to one of the Sisters, "Wow! When was Baby Llama born?" They said, "What baby llama?!" and all went running out to see. I learned then that the llama had been born very shortly before I saw it. What I didn't know was that llamas have an instinct to get up and run with the herd right away so they are ready to move within minutes after birth. I laughed all day, thinking how I had waited and waited for this birth to happen and when it did happen, I did not recognize it. That's a lot like life. At first we don't know what is changing for us; then when it is happening, we often don't trust that it is happening because we are so set on our own idea of how it should be.

Along with staying open to how the future might unfold, rural Americans need to constantly remind themselves and one another of their inner strength. In *The Art of Resiliency,* Carol Osborn encourages her readers to never doubt their inner ability to overcome great obstacles. In a 1999 interview she described resilience as "the ability to get through, get over, and thrive after trauma, trials and tribulations . . . Resilience means that we can be challenged and not break down."

Rural America needs resilience now more than ever. Those who are struggling cannot give up even though the situation may look bleak. Again we can learn from the land's resiliency. I remember being at Mt. St. Helen the first year after that volcano blew, destroying everything alive in its path of hot ash. I was astounded to see beautiful red fireweed already growing among the ashes. I couldn't believe my eyes. I was amazed that something so alive had come out of something so dead.

As Rural America looks to its enduring people and the beauty of the land let us all heed these words of Jesuit paleontologist Teilhard de Chardin:

> God is at work within life; God helps it, raises it up, gives it the impulse that drives it along, gives it the appetite that attracts it, the growth that transforms it. I can feel God, touch God, live God, in a deep, biological current that runs through my soul and carries it with it. The deeper I descend into myself, the more I find God at the heart of my being.

God is with us and is guiding us. God has given us the land, not only for producing abundant food but also as a source of hope. The land is our teacher. Let us be attentive to what is happening within us and around us. Let us be aware of the land's teachings about transformation. There is an elixir, a gift, for rural America beyond the current struggle and pain. We will discover what this is if we let the land teach us.

—*NCRL*, February 23

FOR A BRIEF MOMENT

for a brief moment
early spring rain ceases.
the sun breaks through
grey sky.

> threads of gold,
> thin enough to pierce
> the forest,
> glitter on dewdrops,
> touching the eyelashes
> of blooming forsythia,
>
> making of the yellowed bushes
> a place where beauty
> bows to brilliance,
>
> where everything arrogant
> takes off its shoes
> to stand on holy ground.
>   —*My Soul*, 93

The following three excerpts are from Joyce's book Walk *in a* Relaxed Manner: Life Lessons from the Camino. *At age sixty Joyce didn't know what she was getting into when she began a thirty-seven-day pilgrimage along the Camino de Santiago in northern Spain. Joined by her walking friend Tom, a retired pastor, she learned lessons that can help all of us travel on life's up-and-down journey with grace and lightness.*

WALK IN A RELAXED MANNER

> *The simplicity of resting—*
> *there is much profoundness in that.*
>   —*Khandro Rinpoche*

The biggest lesson I learned on the Camino was that I needed to slow down. It was the most difficult thing to learn. It came to me, as did many of the other lessons, in a slowly awakened way. Had I been more alert during the summer preparation time when I felt harried and hurried, I might have been ready for this challenging teaching.

As it turned out, the lesson came in the early days after we started our walk in Spain. Tom and I both became increasingly tired and disgruntled with our pressured pace during the first week. It was ironic, there we were thousands of miles away from home and work, with seven weeks free from "have to dos" and "don't forgets." We had no lists to make, no phone calls to be returned, no mail to open, no meetings to attend, no requests to acknowledge, no deadlines. Nothing. What a grand opportunity to relax and be released from the pressure of *getting things done.*

Then why, we asked ourselves, were we hurrying and rushing to get to the next *refugio*? Why did we try to keep up with the other pilgrims who were zooming past us at express speeds? What urged us to accelerate our pace and count our miles so precisely? Why did we hesitate to give ourselves adequate time to rest? What was the source of this self-imposed pressure to keep moving faster, to hurry forward to each day's destination?

One major cause of our pushing onward was the need to find housing each night. Every day we started out earlier than some of the other pilgrims who stayed at the same *refugio* but they always caught up and passed us by later on because we walked more slowly. About mid-morning we would hear the clickety-click and the thumpety-thump of metal and wooden walking sticks behind us. Soon these pilgrims (mostly physically fit Europeans accustomed to hiking) would dash past us at incredible speeds. Pilgrim after pilgrim zipped by us on the path. When this happened, I got a sinking feeling Tom and I were the last ones on the road. A growing desire shoved me on to go faster, to enter the race with everyone else. It was obvious to me that we were definitely going to be *left behind* if we didn't *hurry up.* I pressed forward, causing Tom to reluctantly do the same.

Seeing all the other pilgrims hurrying along served as an anxiety raiser because it meant they would get to the *refugios* long before us and be able to claim a bed there. We soon understood there were only two or three *refugios* within the distance of the day's walk. In those places a limited amount of beds was available. *Refugios* did not take reservations so the early birds who arrived first would find a place to sleep that night and we late-comers would not.

Another reason for hurrying was a silently competitive voice inside me growing louder every day. Tom and I gave ourselves a set amount of time to get to Santiago. We figured we needed to walk an average of ten to twelve miles per day in order to arrive there in our allotted time. If we kept to this average mileage each day, we were confident of easily meeting our estimated goal.

I was okay with limiting our miles until the third night when we heard a sturdy German pilgrim announce he had walked thirty miles that day. I felt like a wimp by comparison. Then, when I saw others zooming along at high speeds which took them many more miles per day than us, a voice inside chided that we should do more. While Tom was more comfortable than I with walking slowly, he too picked up the pace. Who would believe a competitive spirit burned and thrived on a pilgrimage—but there it was.

Besides dealing with this self-inflicted stress of comparison, the Camino also challenged me to accept my aging process. At sixty, I simply could not walk as quickly and nimbly as a twenty- or thirty-year-old. I needed to walk more slowly, rest regularly, and make sure my body received good care. Every day the Camino reminded me of my age. Quite honestly, I did not want to appear old, trudging along without the energy of the more youthful pilgrims. My ego wanted to keep up, make a good appearance, show them I could do it. (Another lesson! I took my ego with me, even on the Camino's sacred path.)

Gradually I accepted my diminishing energy. I learned to be at peace with it. I also grew more grateful because the deliberately measured pace helped me slow down inside, causing me to become more contemplative as I walked along. This did not happen the first week, however. During the first week our sense of urgency continued to grow. Each morning we made as early a start as possible. We packed our backpacks faster. If we stopped for mid-morning coffee, we didn't tarry long. When we met other pilgrims we cut our conversations short. When we paused to rest our feet, we kept the stop brief.

Our unspoken motto became: Push onward. Push forward. Push, push, push. Rush, rush, rush.

We soon discovered that the rushing and pushing caused us to lose our enjoyment of the walk itself. We left home in order to experience the freedom of *getting away from it all but* we simply took the tensions with us in new forms. *The place* of our stress changed but we had not changed. We continued to strain and groan under the desires and expectations of achievement and accomplishment—goals which our culture thrives on and implants in us almost from birth.

Finally, Tom and I had a good talk and both agreed the stress of hurrying denied us our inner harmony and the spiritual adventure of the Camino. We decided to slow down. In order to do that we needed to change our attitude and behavior: no more rushing, competing, and worrying. We finally took to heart a significant message that arrived the day before we left for Spain. I received this wisdom in an email from Bernard Thorne, a Servite friar in Ireland. When I was with Bernard at a meeting in Portugal in July, I was astounded to discover he was headed for the Camino two days after the conference. I asked Bernard if he would email some advice to help Tom and me on our walk when he returned from his pilgrimage experience. Bernard promised to do so.

The day after Bernard returned I received a very short note from him saying he had little advice to offer except to tell me that during the first two weeks of his walking he "had a lot of blister trouble." He then went on to describe how he met an old man in one of the *refugios* during the second week. This old man looked at his blistered feet and advised: "Drink more water and walk in a relaxed manner." This bit of counsel made an immense difference for the rest of Bernard's pilgrimage. When he slowed down and drank more water his blisters left and, at the same time, his peace of mind and heart returned.

Walk in a relaxed manner. Much easier said than done. Tom and I were productive-oriented people, the kind you can count on to get things done. Both of us were in church ministry, which we gave ourselves to full-heartedly. (Fool-heartedly too!) Tom was semiretired but still felt inundated with way *too much to do.* As for me, I continually faced stacks of unanswered mail, deadlines for retreat talks and writing, as well as numerous social commitments. The months before I left for Spain I felt constantly frazzled, trying to *get it all done* before I left for almost two months. I'd get one thing finished in the office and ten more items popped up, demanding my attention. This was nothing new. I experienced this pressured approach almost every day, like many other people I knew. These busy colleagues and friends all went through the same thing so I accepted pressing and hurrying as the *normal* way to live if one chose to be responsible, faithful, and successful.

This lifestyle does not work for a physically and spiritually healthy Camino, nor does it work for a truly healthy life anywhere. It leads to anxiety, distress, and discontent. I discovered during my days as a pilgrim that I could not be at peace unless I walked in a relaxed manner both internally and externally. I had to come to terms with why I felt a need to push, to rush, and always to give too much time *to getting somewhere and doing something.*

Was it due to religious and social expectations, the pressures of the job, or my own inherited sense of responsibility? After many days of walking on the Camino I decided it was a combination of all of those things and that it was definitely something I wanted to alter in my attitude and actions. I had to slow down inside, change the messages I gave myself about achievement and responsibility. Walking in a relaxed manner on the Camino was a great catalyst for that attitudinal adjustment.

Once Tom and I decided we wanted to pace ourselves differently, the days on the Camino gradually changed for us. We discovered that our outer action of slowing down our walking also influenced our inner tempo. We grew more peaceful and enjoyed our time with other pilgrims instead of envying their faster walking strides. The beauty of the Spanish countryside took on a deeper color and hue. Its people seemed to grow friendlier by the day. We worried less and were more at home with ourselves and one another.

The wisdom of the old man's advice to Bernard also helped us physically. Slowing down our pace proved to be much easier on our feet. They did not get as heated, which meant they were less likely to form blisters. Our legs felt less tired. We found we could actually walk our daily miles much easier than if we pressed at a quicker pace. The other blessing of going slower was that Tom's easily irritated ankle behaved itself once we stopped pushing so hard.

Another way we stopped hurrying was to take longer rest periods as we made our way westward on the pilgrimage. We basically took three kinds of rests: little ten- to twenty-minute ones throughout the day, longer half-day ones when we ended our walking by 1:00 or 2:00 in the afternoon, and big ones of a whole day when we did not walk at all. We found, eventually, that the rests we enjoyed the most were the times when we walked around five hours and then stopped for the day. These half days provided a welcome relief from the usual hurrying we were tempted to do when we did not get to a *refugio* until 4:00 or 5:00 p.m. or later. Stopping early gave us adequate time to hand wash our clothes, take a shower and nap, buy provisions for the next day, stroll leisurely around the town to see any historical sites, study our guidebook, and make plans for the next day's walk. We tried to give ourselves one or two of these days a week and found that when we did so, there was a noticeable change in our spirits.

Walking in a relaxed manner is challenging. There was just too much "hurry" built up in us through the years to keep us from instantly changing our ways. Whenever we thought we were well established in our new attitude and behavior, one of us would want to go further than we originally agreed. At other times one of us would pick up the pace physically or start voicing concern about whether or not we'd find room at the next *refugio*. We had to constantly give our attention to going slowly in spirit as well as in body. It took effort to be present to the new approach we were birthing and growing as we walked. Tom and I reminded each other of this often by simply saying: "Don't forget: Relaxed manner!" or "Time to stop hoofing it!"

When I came back home from the Camino, I observed how rushing and hurrying and pushing are evident everywhere. Overachievement, competition, comparison, addiction to work and duty, unreal expectations of needing to do more, the obsessive pursuit of having more—all these fall on us as heavy cultural and self-imposed burdens. When these attitudes and messages press in on us, they cause us to lose our harmony and self-satisfaction.

There is far too much hurry and worry in most lives. There never seems to be enough time to complete the daily chores of laundry, lawn care, meal preparations, phone calls, and paying bills, let alone the pressure of other accomplishments that people feel compelled to do. Parents with children involved in an overabundance of activities, health care workers working double shifts, educators saddled with extracurricular tasks, managers with countless meetings, retired people with too much scheduled—these are some of the many people who need to walk in a relaxed manner, but who find their responsibilities and overextensions make it difficult to do.

Undoubtedly, it will take a lifetime for me to fully learn the lesson of walking in a relaxed manner. All too easily I am thrown off balance and lose my peaceful equilibrium. When this happens, I ask myself questions like these: Why am I allowing myself to be stressed? Who and what is most important in my life? What is my motivation for what I am doing? How is my ego influencing the pressure I feel? Am I being overly responsible or too competitive? If I died tomorrow, would what I am doing be of importance? These questions usually help me regain my balance.

I believe with all my heart that it is nigh impossible to walk in a relaxed manner externally unless I walk in a relaxed manner internally. I now know that if I change my attitude and approach to life, I will be encouraged to make decisions that help me slow down the rest of my life. The reverse is also true. If I slow down on the outside, internally I will also relax. I long to be able to say what author Thich Nhat Hanh said: "I am not running anymore; I have run all my life; now I am determined to stop and really live my life."

I still have a tendency to run but I am slowing down more often. I even walk slowly sometimes. Every day is a day to walk in a relaxed manner. I'm getting better at it.

—*Walk*, 51–58

EXPERIENCE HOMELESSNESS

had occasion to visit the city shelter last month where homeless families are cared for. I sat there for a couple of hours, contemplating poverty and destitution.
—Dorothy Day

One of my most embarrassing moments on the Camino occurred the day I tried to use my credit card to obtain Spanish cash. For some reason the ATM machine in front of the bank refused to process the exchange. I went inside to where a handsome man in a stylish blue suit sat at a large desk. He nodded to me when I came in and asked if he could help me with a financial transaction. Then he motioned me to sit down in the chair opposite his desk. I had my backpack on so I slid it off instantly, placing it beside me.

The banker first asked to see my passport for identification. Wouldn't you know, the passport lay at the bottom of my pack. I stood up and began digging around to find the precious item. At that moment I regretted hiding my passport underneath everything for fear of it being stolen. I stretched my short arm inside my pack and struggled to reach around things in order to get way down to the bottom. Impossible. I embarrassingly took some of my items out in order to reach the passport. As I did so, a strong aroma wafted into the room. Goat cheese! I forgot it was in my pack. This provision was great to carry because of its hard texture and durability. Goat cheese also had a very distinct odor which I paid little attention to until I stood before the banker. Oh, how pungent that cheese smelled!

My face became redder and redder as I kept searching for the passport. Finally, my hand touched it and I sighed with relief. As I looked up to hand it to the banker I saw a pasted, thin smile on his dark, lean face. He appeared patient but I spied a bit of disdain. "Hummm," I thought, "he probably wants to hold his nose." I apologized to the banker and again he gave me that silent, pasted smile. There was no doubt in my mind his brain was storing up the scene to retell at the dinner table that night: "This smelly pilgrim with her dirty hiking boots dug into this pack of weird things and, whew, the odor that came from that bag, it was enough to gag me. . . ."

After the banker assisted me with the transaction and politely bid me farewell, I took my pack and walked out the door. I don't know which of us felt more relieved at my departure. As I stood outside on the sidewalk and restored my passport to the bottom of my pack, I had this powerful insight: "I am like a homeless person. This is how people back home see and smell them." Until that morning, I had not tuned into homeless people's humiliation or the superior attitudes hovering over them.

The bank incident preceded several other situations in which I experienced a tiny bit of what it is to be a homeless person. At certain times I felt terribly out of place and inappropriately dressed in my pilgrim attire. I rarely thought of how I was clad or what I looked like except when we walked through large cities and mingled with people wearing lovely clothes. I did not have any "nice clothes" to wear. Around well-dressed people, I looked and felt grubby. Although I showered and washed my clothes by hand at the end of each day's walk, inevitably I looked grimy and smelled a bit grungy when I met someone, especially by later afternoon. I perspired in the hot sun, walked through cow and sheep manure, and stirred up dust on unpaved roads. No wonder I appeared disheveled and smelled slightly offensive.

One Sunday afternoon we walked into Villalcázar de Sirga, site of the impressive, thirteenth-century church of Santa María la Blanca, a historical building of the Knights Templar who guarded the Camino in the Middle Ages. The streets were packed with cars because of a wedding in the church. Tom and I did not know the location of the *refugio* or what time it opened. He went to search out information on housing while I found a spot across from the church to stand and watch his backpack. As I stood there, I leaned back on the wall outside a restaurant.

No sooner did I position myself when customers dressed in their wedding fineries stepped out to depart the restaurant. In no time at all, I realized I was standing in the wrong place. The people cast their glances on me with scowls and dirty looks, as if to say, "Why are you here, you repugnant woman? Go someplace else!" I suppose I did appear a bit out of place with my hiking shorts, dirty boots, lopsided sunhat, and bulging backpack. Still, I did no harm as I stood there waiting. Their disdainful looks pierced me with rejection. Immediately, I thought about homeless folks receiving those same looks much of the time.

On another occasion when Tom and I completed a long day's walk, we looked and smelled anything but pleasant. We needed food for the next day so we went to shop before settling into the *refugio*. Because of our weariness, we chose to save our energy by not taking our packs off and setting them down outside the store. Instead, we walked into the store wearing them. Soon after we were inside, a store clerk followed me up and down the aisles. At first, I naively presumed she wanted to help me find what I needed. I turned and greeted her with "*Hola*" but she responded with a glaring, suspicious look. I was stunned. Then I knew she was following me because she thought I might steal something. I guess I looked "the type" to do so.

The longer I walked on the Camino the more my awareness of the destitute increased. I often felt this way when Tom and I were concerned about finding housing for the evening. We never knew for sure if we would have a roof over our heads or not. Even though money was not a problem, housing locations could be full, or there might not even be a *refugio*, a hostel, or a hotel in which to stay. Sometimes we consoled ourselves by saying, "We can always knock on someone's door and ask to sleep in their garage," or "We can find a park and sleep there." I did meet one pilgrim who slept mostly on church doorsteps or in parks as he walked the Camino. More than once I thought to myself, "What must it be like for a person on the street to try to find shelter for the night?"

Waiting in line for *refugios* to open gave me a sense of how the homeless wait in line at soup kitchens and at shelters. Like them, Tom and I stepped into conditions we could not control once the doors opened. These conditions included dim lighting, sometimes one lone light bulb of 35 watts hanging without a shade in the middle of a room of thirty people, or stairwells and toilet areas with no lighting at all. Like the homeless, we felt relieved to have a roof over our heads even if it meant cramped space in dormitories with dense air, dirty conditions, and grungy mattresses. When we found housing at Portomarín I wrote:

> *Staying at a municipal refugio. I am sitting on the top bunk, on my sleeping bag which is on a mattress with a dirty torn cover. The foam shows through the large rip. There are feathers from the pillow and particles of dirt on the foam and on the mattress cover. On my right, there is a two-pane window. It's filthy. The inside has mudcaked dirt around it. The panes are all smudged and blackened with fly specks. In this room there are 5 bunk beds all situated around the walls, leaving the center with a narrow row of free space.*
>
> *Outside my window, pilgrims sit at the entrance to the refugio, speaking in various languages. They are sit-*

ting on an old stone wall that parallels the entrance. I despise these huge, filthy places. I did not take a shower, just cleaned up a little bit. There is only cold water, two showers that are wide open, two sinks, two toilets. No paper and the floor is totally wet and muddy.

Along with the conditions of the *refugios* we stayed in, we also experienced sleeping in a different place almost every night. Each day we unpacked and repacked, putting each item in its plastic bag and making sure we put everything in the best place for carrying. We did not stay long enough to become familiar with a place. Each night we learned a new route to the toilet and adjusted our body to a different bed.

Special attempts to be kind to us also cost us a bit of our dignity. When we arrived at Arzúa the *refugio* director led us up to the third floor to where single cots, not bunk beds, lined the room. When I looked into the room, I felt overjoyed until I noticed a white piece of paper lying on the beds with the printed message: *gente mayor* (old people). The beds were reserved for elderly pilgrims and the director considered me to be one of them!

Washing clothes also linked me to the homeless. I have often heard refined people remark about the poor, "Well, at least they could look clean." Being clean is not so easy as one imagines. First, we sought the sink designated for washing clothes, waited in line to use it, hoped our soap lasted, hurried so another pilgrim could step forward and begin. Next, we looked for the designated place to hang our clothes to dry. When many pilgrims stayed in the *refugio* and there were only a few clotheslines, or sometimes none at all, we hung our washing on bushes and fences and anyplace that held wet clothes. I can't begin to tell you how excited we felt the two or three times we stayed at a *refugio* that had a washing machine. One even included a clothes dryer. What a joy to have clothes that really felt clean.

Food offered another opportunity to associate my experience with that of the homeless. I never knew hunger the way I knew it on the Camino. Several times we ran out of food and could get nothing to eat for miles. Even when food was readily available it was not always something of our choice. On the fourth night of our trek, on a Sunday, we stopped at Cizur Menor, a little way beyond Pamplona. Until time for the evening meal, we did not know most eating places in Spain close on Sundays. There was nothing open in Cizur Menor. A few places might have been open in Pamplona but that meant walking a long distance back into the city and hunting for one. The owner of the private *refugio* gave us an option of ordering food from a delivery place that remained open in Pamplona. We chose the delivered food after Tom exclaimed excitedly, "Hey, pizza! Let's go for it!" Our mouths salivated with the thought of food different from the usual pilgrim fare. We felt famished by the time the pizza arrived an hour or so later.

When we sat down to eat the pizza, I could hardly take more than a few bites. That pizza was the worst food on the Camino. Even Tom, who always insisted he "could eat anything," was unable to stomach the stuff. We chose not to eat the foul tasting food and couldn't even give it away to other hungry pilgrims! No one wanted it. That experience, and the many days when we waited hours for restaurants to open after a long day's walk, caused me to ask Tom, "How do the indigenous do it—going without food after working hard all day? How do the homeless manage to eat whatever is given to them even when it tastes awful?"

The *refugios* provided breakfast once in a while, which was a special gift because we did not use food from our packs and could save it for later in the day. These breakfasts were mostly white bread left over from dinner the night before. We felt grateful for whatever food the *refugios* offered but we were absolutely elated when fresh fruit or an occasional yogurt or cereal showed up on the dining table in the morning.

Those of us who have access to any and all kinds of food may think hungry people are lucky to have any food at all. In a way, I suppose this is true, but what a pleasure to bite into something delicious, to relish a food that our taste buds enjoy. How wonderful to have food that is not just filling but also nourishing and healthy. Everyone ought to have the option of this enjoyment.

Several months after returning home, I read an article in *The Des Moines Register* about a local church that provided a fish fry at a shelter. Several church members saved their summer's catch and wanted to share it with the homeless. The people on the streets who gathered for the meal raved about how good it tasted. After the easy-to-prepare-and-serve, starchy, thick casserole-type foods usually served, the fish dinner was a banquet for them. One homeless man remarked gratefully, "It's the first time I've eaten fish in two years." Had I not been on the Camino, his comment would have held less meaning for me.

My sparse belongings on the Camino also connected me to the homeless. I guarded my few simple possessions like they were gold, not so much out of fear they would be stolen by other pilgrims but because I didn't want to be without one of my precious items. Each one was vital to my journey. When I lived among the disenfranchised two summers in Appalachia, several times I observed the poor sharing what little they had to help another person in need. On the Camino, I also experienced this generosity. One night when Tom and I initially thought we would have nothing to eat for the evening meal, an eighty-year-old Canadian named Philip offered Tom and me all his food. He insisted we take the half loaf of bread and small chunk of cheese he held out to us, saying, "It's okay. I'm not hungry. I had a big lunch." His gesture of generosity touched me deeply because I knew he must be hungry, too. As it turned out, we found food that evening for all of us but had we not, Philip was willing to give of the little he had.

Late in our journey Tom turned to me and said, "If I had to describe each day of the Camino, I'd name it 'how to survive' day: how to take care of our body, how to feed and house ourselves, how to keep ourselves clean." He pointed out that pilgrims, like the homeless, experience a daily challenge to have their basic needs of life met. I agreed but I also recognized how different our journey was from that of the homeless. Tom and I deliberately chose to eat the simple pilgrim meal at bars and restaurants. We chose to dress as we did and we chose to stay in the *refugios*. Choice is rarely possible for those who have no money, no job, no home.

Our pilgrimage gifted us with only a brief glimpse of the homeless. I do not intend, in any way, to romanticize our Camino experience as I compare it to that of being homeless. The two situations are not the same. However, the Camino did provide a keen awareness and a renewed compassion for the plight of those who live from day to day, who do not know where the next meal or the night's housing will be. The Camino was never a "game" to me. I felt the hunger. I loathed the dirt. I sensed the rejection. Yet, I knew my situation to be only temporary. I knew I could leave the Camino and return to everything the homeless do not have.

This lesson of the pilgrimage continues to provide reflection on my attitude toward undocumented immigrants, homeless wanderers, and all those who are disenfranchised. Not long after my return home, I attended a meeting in downtown Des Moines. As I placed coins in the meter, an unshaven, dirt-encrusted, homeless man with his bundle of belongings passed by me. Normally, I'd have averted my gaze. This time I looked directly into his eyes, smiled, and greeted him with, "Good morning." The homeless man looked surprised by my greeting him as another human being. He grunted a "hi" in return and went on his way. Little did he know how much kinship I felt at that moment.

When Christmas came two months after our return from the Camino, both Tom and I confessed to feeling depressed with the largess of gift-giving and the contrast between the life we experienced on the Camino and the life to which we returned. As we pondered this reality, I realized I was approaching life in a new way. The Camino opened my heart more fully to those who seek the basics of life. I can no longer turn away. I want to remember always their right to have the essentials of life that I have.

The first Christmas after walking the Camino, I decided to buy fewer gifts for those who already had more than they needed. The money I saved went to food pantries and shelters for the homeless. I continue to do this in memory of all those who extended kindness when I walked the long route to Santiago, all those who took me in and offered me a place in their compassion.

I will not forget my own sense of homelessness on the Camino. I want it to influence me forever. —*Walk*, 126–34

LOOK FOR UNANNOUNCED ANGELS

An elderly man appears and, despite our discomfort, he chatters away in Spanish, while offering us some chestnuts. He seems almost like an elemental wood spirit.
—*Marilyn Melville*

It seemed to take forever to walk out of Ponferrada. We left the *refugio* when traffic in the city of 50,000 peaked. We had a hard time finding our way through the busy streets. Most intersections were not marked with the usual Camino symbols of the scallop shell or the yellow arrow. Even when the streets were marked, the shells were usually pressed into sidewalk tiles instead of on the sides of buildings, making it difficult to detect the shells. To add to our frustration, it began to rain. As we moved along the street, we grew anxious because we had not seen a marker in quite some time. We looked up at the buildings, down on the sidewalk and all around for signs. To our relief, we spotted another shell imprinted on the sidewalk ahead of us.

We took about fifteen steps forward when I heard a rough voice behind me say, "This way." A blond-bearded man in a long, flowing, red rain cape motioned toward an alley to the right. On the wall of the alley, I noticed a yellow arrow pointing in that direction. Seeing it, I called to Tom but he missed seeing the arrow and hesitated following. I urged him to come. Then we both quickly turned and followed the silent pilgrim who was already moving rapidly down steep steps toward a park-like area along a wide river.

The tall man's cape blew in the windy rain and he reached out to wrap it closer around himself. He appeared mysterious, a bit sinister almost, as he hurried through the alley and down the steps with his head slightly bowed. I wondered about the wisdom of our decision to follow him on the route. Perhaps it was a ruse to lure pilgrims away for robbery. Several times others, like the French pilgrims, warned us to be wary of those who might want to rob us when we walked through larger cities like Ponferrada.

About the time fear flooded over me, I noticed he was taking us on an alternative path leading along a beautiful waterway lined with trees, a much more pleasant walk than through the busy industrial streets we left behind. His angular body and thin, long legs helped him move swiftly. We almost ran to keep up. We feared if we lost him, we might easily lose the direction of the path because there were few arrows on this route, as well. When we lagged far behind, he slowed his pace, and we were able to keep him in view. The red-caped man looked back once or twice to see if we were following. This pattern of his slowing down and our speeding up continued some forty minutes until we reached the edge of the city where it was obvious the central path lay ahead. Then the silent pilgrim picked up his pace and soon was nowhere to be seen.

Like the two on the road to Emmaus, Tom and I pondered that unusual event. How was it, we marveled as we walked along, that the stranger came by just at the moment of our need? How kind that he called out for us to follow him. What caused him to slow his pace so we could keep up with him? Why did he care enough about us to even bother to show us the alternative route? We both felt a certain mystical aura about the experience, almost as if the man was an angel sent to make our journey easier.

By mid-morning we finally found a place where we could stop for coffee. The rain continued so we took off our wet backpacks and left them outside the front entrance. We stepped inside and to our surprise we saw our "angel." We went over to him and thanked him for his kindness. One of us mentioned how grateful we were that he slowed his pace for us. At this he laughed uneasily and muttered, "Don't read more into this than it is." He followed this by saying it was only his mood that led him to walk slowly.

His comment broke the mystical spell, but I still felt some divine intervention had blessed us. Although the tall man did not believe he was an instrument of God's goodness that day, we certainly did. This incident led me to think about how this sort of experience is actually more common than is supposed. People may not deliberately intend to be an instrument of God but they often are, without their realizing it.

The first time this happened on the journey we were en route to Spain. Because of weather conditions we arrived late into the Newark airport, causing us to miss our overnight flight to Madrid. It was 10:30 p.m. and we had not eaten dinner. We stood at the airline counter trying to understand the complicated directions for getting to our lodging for the night. The ticket agent looked exhausted and there was still a long line of passengers behind us to be reticketed. We jotted down the directions as quickly as possible so we wouldn't increase their waiting. Then we started down the concourse.

Neither of us had a clue as to where we were headed. A porter passed by us, noticed our confused looks, and asked if he could help us out. After a few moments of trying to explain, he said, "Here, follow me" and proceeded to walk with us for ten minutes to an elevator that took us in the right direction. As I turned around to say "thanks," he was already on his way, disappearing around the corner. In that moment, I had a strong sense we would be taken care of on the Camino. Even though I had fears and misgiving in the weeks ahead, I was quietly reassured that night because of this angel-like encounter.

While our red-caped angel appeared mysteriously and helped us out physically, another angel on the Camino surprised me by touching my heart. There were three times when I cried on the pilgrimage. The first time occurred when I experienced a hospitaler at the *refugio* in Tosantos. This *refugio* was one of the most welcoming places on the Camino. Much of this was due to his presence. He was a genuine hospitaler, a robust Spaniard who laughed and smiled as he invited weary travelers in, often extending a warm hug with his greeting. His real name was José but Tom and I always referred to him as *Señor Cantante* (Mr. Singer) because he was full of music.

After most of us arrived in the late afternoon Señor Cantante invited pilgrims to join him in practicing songs for the evening prayer. We practiced several chants and the refrain to a great *pere-grino* (pilgrim) song. His enthusiasm proved contagious. His brown eyes lit up as he introduced various melodies and affirmed our ability to sing the chants beautifully. As he directed us to soften the notes and keep the tempo, he sometimes closed his eyes in such a satisfying manner he looked like he was about to levitate. His sincere warmth easily permeated those of us present.

This enthusiasm extended into the dinner hour. Señor Cantante not only led the singing but he also helped to prepare and serve a massive pot of spaghetti with some carrots in it. An equally huge plastic mixing bowl of greens followed and then pieces of fresh fruit for dessert. He even passed a roll of toilet paper around the table when there were no napkins to be found! The conversation among the thirty or so of us that night rang out with both laughter and meaningful sharing. Much of it was due to the atmosphere Señor Cantante engendered.

After the meal we went up to the third floor where, of all surprises, we discovered a little prayer room off to the side with a tiny door through which we entered. I felt like Alice in Wonderland. The room had old round logs on the ceiling, a thin, tan rug on the floor, and cereal bowls holding semiwilted geranium blossoms in front of a faded hearth. We sat in a circle although there was barely room for all of us. Señor Cantante led us through the same prayer service as at the previous place, only we sang all the refrains plus the pilgrim song he taught us. I was thrilled to be singing, to have some music, because I had missed music so much. Even though my body was dead tired, my heart soared.

I am not sure exactly what this kind hospitaler triggered in my emotional response the next morning. We had been on the road for eleven days and maybe I just needed some attentive comfort and care. I only know that when we prepared to leave, Señor Cantante stood at the door to send us off. I thanked him for his hospitality and he responded by telling me it was a pleasure to do so for people like us. He then reached toward me, cupped my face gently in his hands, kissed me on either cheek, and blessed me with the farewell of "*Buen Camino.*" An unmistakable touch of divine love filled that gesture. I sensed the power of a very special soul touching mine. Tears welled up and fell upon my cheeks. I looked to see that Tom was crying, too. My voice wavered as I bid Señor Cantante farewell in that poignant moment.

As I look back on our Camino days, many unannounced angels came into our lives at just the right time to help us with their considerate care: store clerks, *refugio* directors and volunteers, waiters and waitresses, farmers and city folk, and, of course, all those pilgrims who stepped forth when we needed them most. As I look back in reflection on what happened with our many "angels," I realize how fortunate we were to have someone there for us at the exact moment we needed them.

Since my return from the Camino, others have told me about strangers who offered them solace in a hospital emergency room, unknown people who stopped to help change a flat tire, unnamed persons who reached out to extend help or gave information at precisely the time of greatest need. These anonymous people rarely stayed for very long but their good deeds are tucked away in the hearts of those they assisted.

I have often wondered if people like the red-caped man, Señor Cantante, or the elderly woman knew how much their kindness mirrored divine benevolence. I doubt they did. I doubt that any of us are normally aware of having a profound effect on another unless someone tells us about it. We may do a good deed but unless the events are startling or unusual, they generally fade into life's experience without much of a second thought.

Yet, the slightest of actions may have a great influence on another. Each of us can be an *angel* in some way if we take the dictionary definition of *angel* as our source of description: *a messenger, a spirit or a spiritual being employed by God to communicate with humankind.* And what do these angels communicate? For us on the Camino, they brought the message of God's compassion, kindness, thoughtfulness, and solace. We learned these angels are everywhere if the eyes of our souls are vigilant enough to notice.

The Camino helped me believe in the unique way God moves in our lives through the presence of other human beings who show up at the right time. Even when these strangers are oblivious to how they are an instrument of good, they act in a manner surprisingly beneficial and helpful. We never know when someone we meet might be just the right person we need for the moment. We rarely expect unannounced angels in our midst but, oh, how wonderful they are when they show up to grace us with their gifts.   —*Walk*, 153–60

THE PILGRIM PRAYER

Guardian of my soul,
guide me on my way this day.
Keep me safe from harm.
Deepen my relationship with you,
your Earth, and all your family.
Strengthen your love within me

LEANING ON GOD

Some people lean against fence
posts when their bodies ache from toil.
Some people lean on oak trees,
seeking cool shade on hot, humid days.

Some people lean on crutches
when their limbs won't work for them;
and some people lean on each other
when their hearts can't stand alone.

How long it takes to lean upon you,
God of shelter and strength;
how long it takes to recognize the truth
of where my inner power has its source.

All my independence, with its arrogance,
stands up and stretches within me,
trying to convince my trembling soul
that I can conquer troubles on my own.

But the day of truth always comes
when I finally yield to you,
knowing you are a steady stronghold,
a refuge when times are tough.

Thank you for offering me strength,
for being the oak tree of comfort;
thank you for being the sturdy support
when the limbs of my life are weak.

Praise to you, Eternal Lean-to,
for always being there for me.
Continue to transform me
with the power of your love.

*Which of you walks in darkness and sees no light?. . .
lean on God.*

—*Isaiah 50:4–10*

I came upon an old lean-to on one of my mountain hikes. A few
pieces of wood had been nailed together and set up in a remote
pasture. As I looked at the lean-to, I imaged cattle, horses, and

sheep seeking shelter, finding comfort from the harsh storms that can come so quickly to the high places.

I could also see how we humans need our lean-tos in the storms of life which come upon us when our bodies are too weary to work, our spirits too hurt to struggle, and our hearts too pained to care.

The journey of the human spirit has tiring searches, long stretches of grief and letting go, dark-hearted things that steal the energy from us. At these times we need lean-tos. Our lean-tos can be anyone or anything that brings us a sense of hope, a pause from the pain, a bit of strength to sustain us, a little vision for guidance, a touch of happiness.

We have a wonderful lean-to in God, whose heart continually welcomes us and provides refuge for us. We often have people who stand by us and offer warmth, support, and refuge. Little comforts and glimmers of hope that we do not notice when we are strong become very significant for us when we are weak: a smile, a song, a sunrise, a bird's chirp, a phone call, or a letter. In all these we rest our woes and our weariness and draw strength for our recovery.

We all need lean-tos; we all need to be lean-tos for others. That's the blessing of human love and compassion. There are situations and moments in our lives when we are not strong. We feel weak, downtrodden, and miserable. If we are fortunate, others will stand by us and walk with us. They will wait for us to grow, be patient with our pain, speak encouraging words and listen long hours to us. They will believe in us when our own belief is in shreds. They will love us when our own love has been mired in the dregs of self-pity or confusion. They will be strength for us. They will watch patiently with us until our life begins again.

Lean-tos are not permanent havens; they are temporary but essential shelters when the storms rage around us or inside of us. Becoming too dependent upon others is emotionally unhealthy. We trust others for comfort, support, and vision when our spirit feels weak and visionless, but in the end, we have to do our part,

accept our responsibility, and make our own choices and decisions. It is unfair for us to expect others to do this for us. They
can cheer us on and cheer us up. They can go on believing in us
when we cease to believe in ourselves. But they cannot do our
growing for us.

I'm deeply grateful for the lean-tos I've had in my life. I recall
a good friend who helped me through an extremely hurtful situation. My friend never tried to take away the many negative
feelings this situation caused. He didn't criticize me, or rush me
through the feelings, or urge me to hurry up and get over them.
My friend just listened and listened. I trusted his honesty and
integrity. He asked me good questions. He helped me to gain
greater clarity about my situation each time I spoke with him.

One day when I had complained bitterly about the situation
for the thousandth time (so it seemed), I voiced my concern to
him that I was afraid I'd lose his friendship for all the complain-
ing I'd done. I was afraid he would get tired of hearing my nega-
tivity. His response was wonderful. He asked me if I thought less
of him when he was experiencing life's pain and when he needed
a listening ear and heart. My answer was an obvious no. This
response freed me to continue to lean. I did so for over a year,
until I knew that I was ready to leave the past behind me. I was
much healthier emotionally because I was able to lean on a good
friend when I really needed to do so.

I have learned much from the lean-tos in the life of Jesus. The
more I have been able to get inside his human story, to sense
what his thoughts and feelings must have been, the more I see
how he, too, needed shelter, refuge, and strength from life's
tough situations. He felt the stresses and the struggles that we
feel on our own journeys. He knew what it was to need others.

This is evident in the first chapter of Mark's gospel, where
Jesus is already besieged by those seeking healing. Mark tells
us "they brought to him all who were sick and those who were
possessed. . . . The whole town came crowding round the door"
(Mk 1:32–34). Jesus was surrounded by the painful cries, the

ugly odors of leprosy and other diseased wounds, the fears and the distressed sounds of those who were ill. He heard the screams, seizures, and tortured groans of those who were possessed. The mob of people pressed in as well, trying to see what was happening.

In the verse following this description, we learn about one of his lean-tos: "In the morning, long before dawn, he got up and left the house and went off to a lonely place and prayed there" (Mk 1:35). Here Jesus regained his peaceful center. He leans on the One who can restore his inner strength. Weary and worn-out in body and spirit, he seeks solitude and silence, desiring to be filled and renewed, pouring his heart out to someone he knew he could trust. Jesus learned to entrust his entire person to this compassionate presence.

Jesus leaned on his friends in his grief when he received the news of the death of his cousin John the Baptist. He "withdrew by boat to a lonely place where they could be by themselves" (Mt 14:13). What kind of shelter and comfort did Jesus need and what did he seek from those who were with him? Surely his heart was full of grief and sadness. He undoubtedly sought the comfort of being alone with those who had also known John and who understood how much he hurt.

Jesus also sought the lean-to of friends as he traveled during his ministry. Bethany, the home of Lazarus, Mary, and Martha, was a welcome haven for him, a place where he could kick off his sandals and be at home (Lk 10:38–42). What a wonderful, comforting shelter Bethany must have been for Jesus as the tensions and rejections of his work and teachings increased. Scripture does not give us details, but we can imagine how helpful it was for Jesus to be able to speak of his struggles and his troubles with good friends. Perhaps that is why Jesus felt that Mary's listening was more significant than Martha's dinner plans. Mary's listening presence was a wonderful lean-to for Jesus.

One of the most intense leaning moments of Jesus was in the Garden of Olives (Mt 26:36–46). Jesus goes there in anguish and distress to draw strength for the final hours of his journey.

He yearns to lean on his friends, but they fall asleep. Jesus says sadly to them: "So you had not the strength to stay awake with me . . .?"

While hanging on the cross, Jesus leans on the disciple John. The same disciple symbolically leaned back "close to [Jesus's] chest at the supper" (Jn 21:20). John stands beneath the tortured body of his beloved friend. Jesus sees him there, sees his mother in such pain, and chooses to lean on John by giving his mother into John's care.

It is a tender moment, one that must have comforted Jesus, knowing Mary would not be left alone (Jn 19:25–27).

Sometimes we are forced to lean. We are too weak to go it alone. Jesus experienced this as he fell again and again under the heaviness of the cross. Physically, he could not do it by himself. How humbling for him to see Simon of Cyrene forced to carry the wood for him. Yet, what a gift it was to have the burden lifted from his bruised and bloody shoulders. I think of this when I see people who need others to help them emotionally or physically. It is often a humbling and difficult process to accept the truth of such great neediness.

Jesus learned all his life to lean on the One he came to know in his solitude. That is why his cry from the cross is doubly agonizing to hear: "My God, my God, why have you forsaken me?" (Mt 27:47), that is, "My God, my one from whom I have always gained strength, now, at this desperate time in my life, where are you to lean on?"

Jesus needed his lean-tos, and so do we. For some of us, leaning on God or others is not an easy thing. Our western culture strongly urges us to be independent and self-sufficient. We are supposed to have things under control, to be strong enough to not need anyone else, to not "lose our grip," to "pull ourselves up by our own bootstraps." People hide their sorrow and pain. They do not like to be dependent, even on something physical such as using a cane.

Men, especially, have been encouraged to be tough and to not let the pain show. They usually find it more difficult to lean on others than women do. When we lean, we admit our weakness or our need to be helped. We also recognize the value of another's strength in the face of our own insufficiency.

I recall a man at one of my conferences who voiced his sadness at continually having to appear strong: "I can't let myself fall apart. I've always been taught that I am totally responsible for my family. What if I let them down? What if I fall apart? I can't let my family see my inner pain." I felt such compassion at that moment for all men who have been convinced that it is wrong or irresponsible to lean on others.

Our family history and our personality may also affect our ability to trust others with our pain and hurt. Some ethnic backgrounds encourage too much dependency, while others insist on complete self-sufficiency. I know this from personal experience. My German heritage brings with it a belief that one should always be able to stand alone and get through life without having to lean on others. My heritage says: "If you just have enough courage you can get through anything. Don't ask others for help. Use your own resources. Whatever you do, don't let your weakness be seen or heard outside the family. Swallow the tears, shove the pain aside, and get on with life." Sometimes this heritage is a tremendous blessing, because it helps one to be resilient, to be a survivor. At other times, it is a terrible curse because it means that suffering is endured alone and for a much longer time than is necessary.

I learned the blessing of leaning when I had major surgery. A member of my religious community wanted to be with me but I told her I could manage just fine by myself. She insisted, so I gave in rather reluctantly. I had no idea what it would be like to come out of surgery feeling so helpless and full of pain. What a relief to find her in my room when I awoke from the anesthetic. I really needed to lean on her compassionate presence. She was a comforting strength to me all that day as she sat there with me. I knew she was there for me if I needed her. My first day of recovery would have been much more difficult if she had not been there.

Another reason we might not lean very well is that we may not know and trust God enough. We may dread the thought of being vulnerable—even to God. We may fear what will happen to us if we surrender ourselves to God, or we may find ourselves getting tired of having to lean on God. We'd like to be able to take care of the pain by ourselves. I once saw a cartoon that said, "God, would you help me with this, but make it look like I did it all by myself?"

The Hebrew psalms are filled with images of God as an encircling shield, a shelter, a stronghold when times are difficult, a rock, a fortress, someone who revives our soul and girds us with strength, shelters us under an awning and hides us deep in a protective tent. God is a comfort in illness and a light in the darkness.

What a wonderful opportunity we have to take our struggles to this God and receive encouragement, strength, consolation, compassion, understanding, and full acceptance. I encourage you to identify your lean-tos, your shelters and places of comfort. Identify what keeps you from leaning on God, or others, when you need to.

Take time to notice the lean-tos around you: park shelters, public transportation huts and bus stops, walkers and crutches, umbrellas, awnings, and shade trees. As you see these shelters, remember one of your spiritual shelters and give thanks.

—*May I Dance*, 48–56

CONTEMPLATION

*It is not we who choose
to awaken ourselves,
but God who chooses
to awaken us.*

—*Thomas Merton*

a small frog
floating, splayed out, waiting,
all of her body in the pond
except her goggled eyes,
round buttons of attention
rising above the clear water,

a small frog,
looking, I realize, at me
while I look at her,
both curious
about the other's presence

a small frog
silently attentive,
calling me back to stillness
until I sit without purpose,

content to gaze
with an awakened
sense of wonder

—*My Soul*, 109

3

Cosmos

Pick a flower on earth and you move the farthest star.
—Paul Dirac, Nobel Prize 1933

If one part of the body suffers, every part suffers with it. If one part is honored, every part rejoices with it."
—1 Corinthians 12:26

Gravitation binds everything so closely that alienation is a cosmological impossibility."
—Thomas Berry

The melody of the dance of life has played in Joyce's soul from the time she fed chickens after school and smelled her mother's chicken soup on the stove to the day she looked at blooming forsythia and beheld a place of beauty "where everything arrogant takes off its shoes to stand on holy ground."

These brief moments of awareness of a cosmic mystery led Joyce to discoveries that expanded her adult spirituality. "The most astounding discovery that both awakened and affirmed my early childhood awareness is the fact that I am part of a vast and marvelous dance that goes on unceasingly at every moment in the most minute particles of the universe."

The following selections are from The Cosmic Dance: An Invitation to Experience Our Oneness *(with artwork by Sr. Mary*

Southard). The cosmic dance is a metaphor for the purposeful movement of God throughout the universe, and on the light that shines even in darkness. Just as a sunbeam can never be separated from the sun or from every other sunbeam, nothing can separate us from the Source of our Light or from each other. Shall we dance?

> *We are already one. But we imagine that we are not. And what we have to recover is our original unity. What we have to be is what we are.*
>
> *—Thomas Merton*

WE ARE ONE

little dancing feet full of energy
enlivening every particle of the universe,
tiny feet skipping, hopping, jumping,
strong feet stomping, jiggling, prancing,
leaping to a rhythm that defies regulation.
airy, bright feet of sailing stars,
wrinkled, callused feet of clay cliffs,
waxy, webbed feet of succulent leaves,
fast flowing feet of winding rivers,
endless feet of unobserved tree roots,
soft feet of every form of fetus.
with an eye as fresh and delicate as birth,
sneak a peek as each pulsing part of life
comes dancing, whirling, weaving,
secret neurons, veiled photons, hidden electrons,
whirling, skipping, pirouetting,
forming a circle of oneness with each other.
if your ear is keen enough, you will hear
their insistent, silent symphony,
moving freely in chasubles of beauty.
receive the music of their secret unity
as they glide within each other's life,
unaware of barriers built by static minds.
slip off the glaucoma of your heart
and revel in this signal beauty
dancing passionately
in the universe, and trembling in each atom.
—*Cosmic Dance*, 15–16

Energy is the substance of life, the unrelenting well-spring of pure possibility, escalating and undulating as in a great cosmic dance.

—*Diarmuid O'Murchu*

There is such power in the cosmic dance. Each time I resonate with this energy I sink into my soul and find a wide and wondrous connection with each part of my life. I come home to myself, feeling welcomed and restored to kinship with the vast treasures of Earth and Universe. I am re-balanced between hope and despair, slowed down in my greedy eagerness to accomplish and produce no matter the cost to my soul, beckoned to sip of the flavors of creation in order to nourish my depths.

When I was young, I presumed that each element of the universe was isolated from the other. My desk was a solid object and separate from me. The lilacs were separate from the garden fence. The cattle were separate from the fields in which they grazed. All was distinct, apart from the other. It was not until much later in life that I read the theories of great scientists such as Neils Bohr, Albert Einstein, Max Planck, Arthur Koestler, and others who developed the understanding that everything in existence consists of light and heat particles or waves that are constantly in motion.

These scientists referred to the light and heat of each piece of existence as packets of energy which were termed "quanta." It is these energy packets that are alive, interactive, and interrelated to one another, always moving, always involved in a constant dance of existence. They may look like they are self-contained in an animal, a human, a seashell, or a piece of metal but their patterns of movement can and do flow freely as in a dance. They can be changed and transformed by being in relationship to other particles of existence.

This patterned, or chaotic, movement of quanta is a mysterious process of motion in which there is constant change and interaction happening. Things are always in relationship to one another. One thing is affecting something else. Kentucky farmer and author Wendell Berry put it this way: "The world that environs us, that is around us, is also within us. We are also made of it; we eat, drink and breathe it; it is bone of our bone and flesh of our flesh."

The magic and the mystery of this cosmic dance confirmed what I had sensed in my youth—that there was some sort of energy in what I experienced as the beauty and wonder of creation. This energy fed, nurtured, and resonated in my soul, wordlessly, giving me a sense of oneness with what I experienced. What I did not know is that this spiritual sense of being intimately connected to all of creation was also grounded in scientific discoveries.

Scientist Elizabet Sahtouris describes the beginnings of Earth in this amazing, interactive way:

> *Particles, or subatomic particles, are the tiniest whirling packets of pure energy from which all matter—all the stuff of the universe—is made. The whirling energy of particles created a new force, or forces, among particles, so that when early cosmic particles passed close enough to each other to attract each other, some of them held together as simple atoms. We can imagine this as rather like people dancing, attracting each other when close enough to whirl about each other. . . .*

Many events and experiences lead me to glimpses of this marvelous cosmic dance. They are not necessarily "big moments." Oftentimes these glimpses are simple, quiet, unassuming ones. Usually they begin with the help of my five external senses. Maybe I am sitting in the park and I see a pair of robins perched on a thin mulberry branch, or walking down a city street and a wild gust of wind sweeps by my face. Perhaps I stand still for a bit by a clump of trees, breathing in the freshness of the pines. I might be hurrying through a store and get caught up with the vulnerability of an elderly couple helping each other navigate through the crowds. It might be the simple gesture of sipping a cup of freshly brewed coffee or brushing rain off my coat. Each of these moments invites me into an awareness of the unspoken dance of energy connecting me to what I am experiencing. I sense for a moment that there is a hidden bond between myself and what is around me.

The cosmic dance is not limited to any one time or place. I have discovered it in the night sounds of the Liberian bush and in the crash of the magnificent waves against the cliffs of the southern Australian shore. I've sensed its power when walking amid the trees along the Black River in Northern Ireland and at the shrine of the goddess Kanon, south of Tokyo. I have beheld the dance in the laughter and cries of little children on airplanes and have seen it in married couples' eyes as they look with love and good humor. I have danced with this energy of life in celebrations and rituals with women's groups in many countries and alone on my hikes in the Rocky Mountains and while sitting in my own back yard.

I now truly believe that I can experience this hidden dance everywhere, in a city full of tall buildings as well as in a small town where one can easily commune with trees and sky. I can know it whether I am driving on a busy expressway or down a narrow road past trim New England farms. Recognition of the cosmic dance happens in deliberate moments of contemplation but it also rises up surprisingly, like a breaching whale splashing high in the sea, commanding one's full and unexpected attention.

Wherever and however I join with the cosmic dance, it jogs my memory and gives me a kind of "second sight," a glimpse of the harmony and unity that is much deeper and stronger than the forces of any warring nation or individual. My trust that good shall endure is deepened. My joy of experiencing beauty is strengthened. My resolve to continually reach out beyond my own small walls is renewed. The energy that leaps and twirls in each part of existence commands my attention and draws me into a cosmic embrace. I sense again the limitless love that connects us all. I come home to that part of myself that savors

kinship, births compassion, and welcomes tenderness. I re-dis-
cover that I am never alone. Always the dance joins me to what
"is."   —*Cosmic Dance*, 15–19

STAR-BREATH

I lie awake on summer's greening grass
soon to be soft with evening's dew.
I lie expectantly, silently,
waiting for a presence to breathe upon me.

With the first sigh of the evening star
my heart responds to a distant touch,
a wisp of recognition, a waft of joy.

Life-giving breath of the galaxies
sails through the heavens
into my gasping, yearning spirit,
uniting me in the marrow of my soul.

Star-breath washes over me
like god-breath
filling the soul of a new creation,
awakening my soul's withered bones,
lifting them into lightness and dance.

I open my small, isolated self to the stars
and am once again healed of my disparity,
the falsehood of a separate identity.

Infusing star-breath fills my soul
with eternal oneness.
My being absorbs the star's sighing,
and I enter into the easy sleep
of endless communion.

—*Cosmic Dance*, 43

WE SIMPLY CANNOT LIVE APART
FROM ONE ANOTHER

The fog has settled in the woods bringing with it a quiet flow of mystery. A red-tailed hawk flies low through the trees, noiseless in her breakfast flight. I stand at the kitchen sink, gazing silently through the window. A tender peace webs its way inside of me as I peer into the milky haze. I feel enfolded in a love much greater than my own. At this moment I lean back in memory and catch a hint of what I knew long ago when I was a small child living on a farm in rural Iowa. It is the melody of the cosmic dance playing in my soul since those early days, a song that has never stopped singing in me.

I never would have named this exquisite bonding quite that way when I was young. But the truth of it was in my bones as I lay on my back looking up at the sparkling sky full of stars and slept overnight on the dew-laden lawn. This hidden dance played in my soul as I fed the chickens each day after school or went down to the barn, climbed the tall ladder to the hay mound, and tossed down hay to the cattle below. This same dance skipped in my spirit when my father, brothers, and I harvested oats and corn. It was there in my mother's presence as I came into the farmhouse on wintry evenings and smelled her delicious chicken soup on the stove. I sensed this dance when I worked with her in the vegetable garden on hot, humid summer days.

As I grew older I lost some of my awareness of the cosmic dance for awhile. I was too focused on a busy life of work and often failed to notice the unspoken mystery in all of creation. But eventually I made some startling discoveries—three of them—and they have changed my life forever. The first of these is the amazing revelation that I am made of stardust, that every part and parcel of who I am materially was once a piece of a star shining in the heavens. The second discovery is that the air I breathe is the air that has circled the globe and been drawn in and out by people, creatures and vegetation in lands and seas far away. But the most astounding discovery that both awakened and affirmed my early childhood awareness is the fact that I am part of a vast and marvelous dance that goes on unceasingly at every moment in the most minute particles of the universe.

I picture these invisible particles that compose every piece of existence as having little dancing feet. Something as sturdy as a boulder does its own boulder dance but it also weaves in and out of the dance of the soil, the dance of the worm, the dance of the wolf. The stone, the soil, the worm, the wolf, cannot be contained. They dance with everything else that "is." What a marvel, to think that each cell of my body is part of an intricate interweaving of the dynamic life of creation!

These discoveries were revealed to me through workshops, conferences, and books on quantum physics, theology, spirituality, and holistic health, as well as literary pieces, including poetry. These teachers were building on the studies, insights, intuitions, and experiences of wise people of the past whose work I had read and relished, such as Teilhard de Chardin, William Wordsworth, Walt Whitman, Rachel Carson, and Emily Dickinson, who sensed the cosmic dance years earlier. I read and resonated with the current thought and explorations of Thomas Berry, Beatrice Bruteau, Fritof Capra, Annie Dillard, Elizabeth Dodson Grey, Joanna Macy, Mary Oliver, Sally McFague, Diarmuid O'Murchu, Elisabet Sahtouris, Rupert Sheldrake, Brian Swimme, Margaret Wheateley, Gary Zukav, and numerous others who were speaking a similar language while using a great diversity of images and literary styles.

No one person has been able to fully communicate this amazing dance of life to me, but Thomas Merton comes close with his description in *New Seeds of Contemplation*. Merton's use of the phrase "cosmic dance" set my heart singing. When I read it, I felt my early childhood experience of the inner dance being echoed and affirmed:

> *When we are alone on a starlit night; when by chance we see the migrating birds in autumn descending on a grove of junipers to rest and eat; when we see children in*

*a moment when they are really children; when we know
love in our own hearts; or when, like the Japanese poet
Bashō we hear an old frog land in a quiet pond with a
solitary splash—at such times the awakening, the turning inside out of all values, the "newness," the emptiness
and the purity of vision that make themselves evident,
provide a glimpse of the cosmic dance.*

There are so many ways in which the cosmic dance becomes
evident. Space explorers discovered this oneness in a visual way
as they marveled at the astounding beauty of our planet from
17,000 miles away. When they gazed at Earth sailing through
space, they realized in a deeply profound way the power of its
being "home" for all dwelling there. After Jacques-Yves Cous-
teau spoke with some of these space explorers, he commented:
"From their exceptional journeys, they all came back with the
revelation of beauty . . . They all emphasize that our planet is
one, that borderlines are artificial, that humankind is one single
community on board spaceship Earth."

We simply cannot live apart from one another. Our ecosys-
tems are key reminders of this intricate ballet of interaction. One
of the reasons our trees are such precious commodities is that
they breathe for us. They give us the oxygen we need by puri-
fying the air. Their roots absorb water and carry it to the leaves
where it comes in contact with the carbon dioxide that we have
exhaled and which the tree needs for its growth. (An acre of
healthy trees can produce enough oxygen for eighteen people.)
Forests also influence our lives by cooling and humidifying the
air as the trees release moisture through their leaves and needles.
We need trees and trees need us, it is as simple, and as marvelous,
as that.

Those who spend significant time with the creatures of our
planet also discover the power and beauty of the cosmic dance of
oneness. Scientist Jane Goodall studied chimpanzees for almost
forty years. A large portion of her life was spent in the Gombe
wilderness of Tanzania. She sat in steaming sun and pouring

rain, sometimes slept on the forest floor at night, as she watched for hours and hours. What she discovered was that "together the chimpanzees and the baboons and monkeys, the birds and insects, the teeming life of the vibrant forest, the stirrings of the never still waters of the great lake, and the uncountable stars and planets of the solar system formed one whole. All one, all part of the great mystery. And I was part of it, too."

The soul of the world and our own souls intertwine and influence one another. There is one Great Being who enlivens the dance of our beautiful planet and everything that exists. The darkness of outer space, the greenness of our land and the blue of our seas, the breath of every human and creature, all are intimately united in a cosmic dance of oneness with the Creator's breath of love.

—*Cosmic Dance*, 9–12

KINSHIP WITH CREATURES

Give praise to the Beloved,
all the earth,
all that swim in the deep,
And all the winged ones of the air!

Give praise all mountains and hills,
all trees and all minerals!
Give praise all four-leggeds
and all that creep on the ground!
—*PS 148 (Nan C. Merrill, Trans.)*

Insects, birds, mammals, mollusks, and more,
my sisters and brothers, living beings,
each of us seeded in Earth's sacred womb.

We drink from the same running waters,
find nourishment from the same sun-fed soil,
unique cells dancing and tumbling in form,
separate yet connected, declaring we are one.

I applaud the bull snake's brave shedding of skin,
cheer the sand cranes dancing their mating games,
laugh with the kookaburra singing her song,
walk at dawn near young foxes leaping with life,
warn mosquitoes to keep away from my skin,
admire busy spiders spinning intricate webs,
listen to singing locusts and frogs harmonizing.

I stroll in the park with butterflies and bees,
work in the garden with ladybugs and moles.
I wear sheep's wool, drink cow's milk,
enjoy the omelets of eggs and pour
the fruit of bee's hard work into my tea.

Heard, or unheard, their melody is near.
Seen, or unseen, creatures are with me
as we sleep in the same great arms of Earth,
and sip from the same large river of life.

* * *

*The fifth kingdom is that of the animals, multicellular
heterotrophs with developed capacities for digestion.
The largest subgroup of those classified is that of the
insects, some eight hundred and fifty thousand species. There are at least five hundred thousand species
of round worms and forty thousand vertebrate species.
Among the vertebrates there are nine thousand bird species, six thousand reptile species, and four thousand five
hundred mammalian species.*
        —Brian Swimme and Thomas Berry, The Universe Story

Imagine all the creatures that have lived on Earth since the
beginning of time, both those now extinct as well as those whose
life forms still dance on the planet. The diversity and variety of
creatures on land and in the sea is astounding. My experience
of the beauty, wildness, instinctual wisdom, compassion, humor,

cleverness, and freedom of creatures has enriched my life with kinship and companionship beyond measure.

Humans throughout the ages have been fascinated with the creatures of our planet. Historic sites like the limestone cliffs in southern France contain paintings and drawings of bison, rhinos, leopards, bears, oxen, lions, horses, and other creatures that existed during the Ice Age over 35,000 years ago.

My earliest recollection of a creature I felt kin to was our farm dog, Pal, a large friendly collie. I loved Pal and hurt for him when he would whine and moan with the noise of thunderstorms that pained his sensitive ears. Pal was a loving playmate, letting me ride on his back when I was little, and was always very protective.

Creatures are beautiful. I will never forget the hundreds of starfish that came in with the tide on Elephant Island, south of Anchorage. As I waited for the tide to return them to the sea, I was astounded at the great variety of colors and sizes of the starfish with their stippled and striped designs. I felt like Alice in Wonderland walking among those gifts of the deep with their bright orange, pink, green, blue, yellow, and purple bodies.

I am especially enthralled with creatures in the wild. Their presence unglues my little world of control and lets me breathe in the beauty and freedom of their untamed presence. Watching herds of rutting elk thundering out of the forest at dusk in Colorado, sighting a black bear in a ponderosa pine tree, hearing coyote yips in the night, coming across moose munching away in a marsh in Maine, kayaking with sea otters by my side and porpoises at play in the sea, hearing the swish-swish of fruit bats over my tent, sighting an emu in the tall grass of Australia, all these have been marvelous moments for me.

Creatures have brought me laughter and admiration of their astute and clever traits. One night I went to the porch and saw a large raccoon standing on his tiptoes pulling the bird feeder down on the branch, sucking out the seeds. I shooed the raccoon away and raised the feeder higher. The next night I looked out and saw the same raccoon standing on tiptoes, again eating from the feeder. Up above him was another raccoon holding down the branch for him!

Creatures can be very compassionate. Elephants mourn the death of their own. Certain horses are known to have intuitive skills whose presence is healing for humans with pain. Some dogs and cats are attached to their owners and often enter a grief-like depression when a beloved owner dies. There are numerous situations where dogs give their lives for their owners or sit by their sickbeds, never leaving their side. A bat was described in the *National Geographic* as "being a midwife" to another bat who did not know how to give birth. The pregnant bat was hanging upside down and the other bat came beside her and demonstrated how to hang upwards so the baby could slip out.

Female creatures have immense mothering qualities. In a terrifying death experience, a bird caught in the Yellowstone Park fire was found petrified in the ashes, perched at the bottom of a tree where she had instinctively gone to try to save her babies. When the ranger moved the dead bird with a stick, he found three tiny chicks still alive under their dead mother's wings.

Sometimes I have to face my fear when entering a creature's world, like hiking in areas where there are mountain lions and bears, or like the day I walked on a trail in northern Minnesota and a hawk, protecting the nest of a newborn, dive-bombed me again and again. (I had never had such big wings whoosh so close to my head!) Or the time a kangaroo came out of the bush, fulfilling my wish to see just such a one. I coaxed him near to me and then he came too close for comfort, sniffing me from foot to head, even touching my cheek with his mouth. I held my breath, wondering if he intended to bite me, but he was just a very curious creature.

Not all creatures I've known have been far from home. Equal delight and teachings have come to me from those in my own back yard and down the street. I have touched a newly born fawn sleeping on the side of a bike path, watched the amazing movement of garter snakes, found comfort from a hoot owl, listened to geese honking in the sky, discovered a possum in a bush by the porch, sat long watching a squirrel gathering dry leaves in his mouth as he made his winter nest, had monarch butterflies sit on my head and spiders spin insistent webs in my house.

I admire the resiliency and inherent wisdom of creatures. The golden plover flies 8,000 miles from Argentina to nest and hatch her young in northern Canada. The caribou have only 3 months to eat enough vegetation to last them through the rest of the year and the female caribou knows that she needs not only green grass and leaves, but also tree bark which provides calcium for her calf.

Migratory creatures teach me that what I need for my life is deep within me if only I will listen. Each season Pacific salmon search for the stream of their birth. They swim intensely until they reach that place where they spawn and begin new life before they die.

Monarch butterflies go to central Mexico each winter, going through several generations of dying and birthing before they once again reach their northern home in the spring. Honeybees find their way back to the hive and ants to the hill. Loggerhead turtles crawl away from sand dunes where they are born and swim directly toward an ocean they have never seen before. The little blackpoll warbler flies from its home in Nova Scotia to South America and manages to come back home again.

Creatures are simply amazing. I feel humbled by their courage and their wisdom. How glad I am for the oneness I have with them.

—*Cosmic Dance*, 71–74

ENTERING THE PAIN OF ANOTHER

Compassion means to come close to the one who suffers . . .
A compassionate person says, "I am your brother;
I am your sister; I am human, fragile, and mortal, just like you . . .

*We can be with the other only when the other ceases to
be other
and becomes like us.*

—*Henri Nouwen*

Native Americans have a saying that we must walk a mile in
someone else's moccasins in order to know what that person is
experiencing. When someone I know and care about is in pain
I can readily walk in their moccasins and extend compassion to
them but how much more challenging it is when the "suffering
one" is part of a person or group whom I consider either an
enemy or a separate entity. This was never so clear to me as
when I entered a side chapel in the beautiful Imperial Cathedral
in Aachen, Germany. A touching statue of Mary, the Mother of
Sorrows, with seven swords piercing her heart, was the center-
piece of this chapel. I sat there for some time, aware of a presence that was unusual and filled with palpable, unspoken grief. I
wondered why I felt it so strongly there.

It was not until later that I discovered the chapel was dedicated
to the mothers of those who had lost their sons and daughters
fighting as Nazis in WWII. I was stunned and felt great remorse.
Why had I never considered these grieving women whose heart-
ache was all as great as those who had lost sons and daughters
fighting for the Allies? It was, of course, because I had never
allowed myself to think of them as part of my cosmic life. I had
never allowed myself to enter into their pain. I had kept them at
a great distance from myself.

A pastor once said that every CEO should have to work in a
packing plant or at a common job for awhile, like every physi-
cian should have to be a patient. These comments came after an
article about a news anchor who was described as being a smug,
cold-hearted person until his four-year-old daughter developed
leukemia. Suddenly he saw how precious life was and what people had to cope with when they were going through tough situations. Now, when he does interviews and stories, he approaches
hurting people with much greater understanding and kindness.

He said he now realizes the immense value of loved ones and what it is like to suffer the loss of them.

When we enter into the suffering of others we enter into the cosmic dance of their pain. It is a tender dance of tears inviting each of us to enter it with compassion for our brothers and sisters everywhere. When we draw near to those who suffer, we enter into this cosmic dance in a deep and powerful way. We embrace mystery and enter into a compassionate love that stretches far beyond our own heart, joining with the One Great Heart that beats endlessly in our vast universe.

—*Cosmic Dance*, 103

* * *

BEHOLD THIS NEWBORN CHILD

Each time a child is born,
particularly after a grandparent dies,
we sense that life goes on.
All is not lost.
There is a deep resilience,
stronger than the grasp of death.

The babe is lifted high
toward the welcoming stars,
a young life
with just a kernel of ripening,
a new resident
in the heart of existence.

All those gathered proclaim:

"Behold, behold, this newborn one!
Let us nurture and keep alive
the sacred mystery of hope
hallowed in this young one's heart.
We sow our dreams of a future

in this freshly birthed being.
We give our loving promise
to guide and guard this child.
Always we will remember
our oneness in the dancing cosmos."

The stars say not a word.
They bow in reverence
to this creature,
whose adult hands will hold
power enough
to blow up a planet,
or seed a waiting garden.

The stars smile,
for they too have hope,
and night
turns toward the dawn.

* * *

Faith in the future is not dead in our hearts. Better still, it is this hope, deepened and purified, which seems bound to save us.
                                        —*Teilhard De Chardin*

When difficulties and misfortune occur there is always the possibility of becoming bitter, hostile, and fearful. On the other hand, there are those who gradually move beyond the overwhelming loss and come to accept hope in their hearts, trusting they will get through the pain and find some kind of positive growth because of what they have experienced. It is true that some things can never be recovered. Loved ones die, accidents cause permanent impairment, species are terminated, natural resources are gone forever. Yet, I believe in hope. My own experience, along with many wounded people who have shared their stories of subsequent growth and healing with me, has convinced me of the necessity of having hope.

I also believe in the power of hope because I have seen Earth survive terrible blows and recover from significant distress. Amid the pain and struggle, the raw wounds of violence and the poisonous harm being done to our planet and to individuals, there are numerous reasons to continue to have hope in the future. A huge amount of goodness rests in the hearts of humankind and much resilience shines through the innermost part of creation.

The yearning toward life is strong and deep in nature. The pattern in creation is one of transformation: out of death comes life. The seasons teach us this as do many other aspects of nature. A dry, brown seed is pressed into a dark space of soil and there it gestates into a new green shoot. An old saguaro cactus with many holes in the arms and trunk lives on and provides a habitat for a variety of creatures. Bushes of green beans given up for dead in the dry garden blossom again after an inch of rain. A three-legged doe, the fourth leg broken and held high, births two young fawns and nurtures them. A flooded cornfield yields a generous crop the following year. Fireweed grows on a mountainside after a devastating fire. Determined grass pushes its way up through the cracks of a concrete parking lot. A green shoot emerges out of a dead tree stump.

Humans also experience the power of transformation. A pregnant Mozambique woman is caught in a raging flood. She spends three days in a tree where she not only survives but also gives birth to a healthy child while in that tree. Others in harsh situations also make it through them. People with serious illness, thwarted dreams, lost jobs, violated bodies, trampled spirits, and grief so deep it penetrates to the core of the soul, gradually return to a sense of peace and acceptance. Those who lose homes in floods, fires, or earthquakes slowly put the pieces of their lives back together. It may take a long time but something deep inside tells them they must go on, that there is more of life yet to live. The voice of hope tells them they can move on into the future. It asks them to trust in the possibility of unfolding happiness even if they can never reclaim what has been lost.

We often do not know until years later how something seemingly hopeless might positively influence the future. Roger and Mary Williams, founders of Rhode Island, were buried side by side in a grave close to where an apple tree was planted. Many years later the local residents wanted to exhume the bodies and bury them with honor but when they excavated the graveside they discovered that the bodies had completely decayed, even the bones. The roots of the apple tree had fed on the phosphorus of the decaying bones and changed the human substance into food for the tree. Even in death, life goes on to nurture the future. Hope prevails.

A new consciousness of how we need to treat Earth and humankind continues to grow and widen. There is a greater awareness of how Earth has been harmed and there is a stronger desire to help her heal from this harm. More individuals are recycling materials, adopting stretches of roads and highways to keep them litter-free, planting trees, using natural resources with greater care and conservation. People are coming closer to nature by gardening, hiking, and other outdoor activities. Legislators are passing environmental laws. Numerous national and international organizations are raising issues and writing charters about systemic changes and attitudes that are needed in order to protect and save our planet.

Farmers are using contour cultivation, hillside terracing, crop rotation, and minimum tillage while conservation corps are reconstructing prairies and wetlands to prevent flooding and protect topsoil. Cities are developing parks, financing recycling programs, and saving "green space" to guard the land from urban sprawl. Environmentally conscious industries are creating new products that use less of Earth's precious resources and others are taking greater care with the disposal of toxic refuse. Much, much more needs to be done to raise awareness, alter attitudes, and change behaviors on behalf of our planetary home but positive beginnings are being nurtured.

There are many who work for the good of our world. This solidarity is an important part of hope, reminding us of our shared values and dreams. Russian cosmonaut Oleg Makarov reflected on how, from outer space, it was easy to see our external solidarity, to view Earth not as many separate, distant countries but as "one touchingly small sphere." From out there he saw our unity.

Teilhard de Chardin named our internal unity when he wrote: "We are all of us together carried in the one world-womb." This solidarity with all that exists is a great source of hope. In this amazing web of oneness there is the unique beauty, power, and resilient dynamism of an interwoven existence. Our oneness in the great dance of life is a tremendous strength. It urges us to live and act in ways that are beneficial for all. It tells us that a sustainable future is possible, one in which everything and everyone lives in harmony, assured of a safe environment in which to grow and mature. We cannot give up hope. We need to foster a deep assurance that the beauty, joy, and nourishment that Gaia, our beloved Earth, offers us will continue far into the future.

I once walked in ankle-deep water across the small, narrow source of the great Mississippi River in northern Minnesota. As I did so, I thought of the myriad streams and tributaries that join to make a wide, vigorous river. Like that river, everyone and everything is joined in the dancing water of the cosmos. Individually we are small rivulets but united we are a mighty river held in one great embrace by the Source of All Goodness. Together we are strong. Together we have hope. Together we will grow. Together we will co-create a world that dances in harmony and love. —*Cosmic Dance*, 111–14

WALKING WITH THE AGED

you thought you were
doing her a favor,
taking her, cane and all,

on the walk
through the deep woods,
helping her move along
November paths
carpeted with remnants
of summer's finery.

you thought nothing
of what she would bring to you
until she paused
at the creek's edge
and asked,
"Do you think our grandchildren
will get to see this beauty?
I love all this so much.
I take nothing for granted."

you eased up on your thoughts
about you being the one to do the giving,
but she wasn't finished.

down the slope, across the creek,
she cried, "Look, bittersweet,
there on that far branch!"
how many times had you walked
that timeless wooded path
and never saw? too fast to see.

it was then you knew
you were definitely not the one giving
and decided
it was time to receive.

—*Cosmic Dance*, 94

ONE STRONG STAR

I stand gazing at the cold winter sky,
thirty minutes after midnight
on the first day of the new year.
What I see catches my heart
and draws me into profound hope.

There in the black winter sky
one strong star sings a silent melody,
illuminating the heavily clouded heights
with a powerful, assuring presence.
I hear it calling to every human soul
whose life yearns for something more.

One strong star sends a brave song
to those who doubt their own courage.
It shines for the soreness of the planet
and for all who die daily
in their coffins of discouragement.

I stand gazing at that single star
resonating with the shining message:
none of us need doubt our ability to survive.
Hope comes in little ways,
it only takes one shining star,
one faithful friend,
one wisp of inspiration,
one touch of creation's beauty,
one deep sip of love,
to keep the illumination alive in us.

In the snow-laden clouds of the first day
of the new year
I bow to the heavens and turn homeward,

grateful for the quiet in my heart,
and for the singing of a lone star
sending strength
to every corner of the cosmos.
—*Cosmic Dance*, 123

A PIECE OF LIGHT

As the sun rose, it filled me until I thought I was all light
and there was nothing left of what I once called ME.
Then suddenly I saw below at the water's edge
another sister of light. My light streamed out to her.
Her light flowed back to me and we were one in the light.
—*Macrina Wiederkehr*

There is a piece of light in all of us,
easily seen in the wise Thomas Berry
longing to heal the wounds of our planet,
in Dorothy Day who embraced the poor,
and Mahatma Gandhi, fighting for peace
with the weapon of nonviolence.

There is a piece of light in all of us,
the grandmothers and grandfathers,
children orphaned by AIDS and war,
the feeble, the lame, the disheartened,
the successful as well as the searcher.

There is a piece of light in all of us,
maybe hidden or buried with pain,
perhaps pushed in the corner by shame.
It is there in the arrogant, the hateful,
racists, torturers, and abusers,
and ones who are willing to kill.

Seen or unseen, the light is there,
ready to kindle, eager to expand,
refusing to be tightly contained.

As soon as the tiniest space is allowed
it quickly emerges, floods outward,
illuminating the darkest of places.

One single candle lights a little dark space.
Many candles light a world full of people
desperately in need of each other's glow.
Each lone light makes us stronger
when we all stand together.

—*Cosmic Dance*, 85

SHE SAW CHRIST IN ALL OF THEM

*Not only was Christ in every one of them, living in them,
dying in them, rejoicing in them, sorrowing in them—
but because He was in them, and because they were here,
the whole world was here too, here in this underground
train; not only the world as it was at that moment, not
only all the people in all the countries of the world, but
all those people who had lived in the past, and all those
yet to come.*

—*Caryll Houselander*

The beauty and variety of people consistently bring joy and
challenge to my life. All I need do is to sit in a busy airport for a
few hours to know there are people of all sizes, shapes, and skin
color, filled with diverse philosophies and values. One thing I
have felt confident about for a good portion of my life is that it
is mainly on the surface that we are different. We are not nearly
as separate as we sometimes feel ourselves to be. Underneath
our supposed differences we experience many similar emotions,
longings, hopes, and dreams. The cosmic dance goes on in each
and every one. It is the externals of appearance and behavior
that divert our attention from the inner radiance and dynamic
goodness within every being.

I was on the tram in the Dallas airport one day and all of
us were standing or sitting quietly, avoiding eye contact and

conversation with one another. Then an elderly man who was holding his wife's hand spoke. He told us they were traveling to celebrate the birthday of a special granddaughter. One person wished them well, then another spoke about it being her 40th birthday that very day. Many "happy birthdays" rang through the air. Soon we were all caught up in the conversation, laughing and enjoying the moment. As the tram came to a stop I realized that in our brief space of time we had discovered our oneness. As we stepped off the tram, however, we all pretended once again that we were isolated individuals and hurried away to catch our flights.

Another time that a stranger led me back to my oneness with humanity was while bathing in the hot springs south of Tokyo. While I sat there seeping in the comfort of the soothing waters, a thin, wrinkled, elderly Japanese woman continually looked at me with an intent curiosity. Later, when we had both emerged and dressed, I sat in a chair waiting for my companions. Quietly this same woman came up to me with a little smile. In her delicate hand she held out a tangerine for me. I smiled in return and opened my hand to receive the gift. In that gesture of giving and receiving, I felt a leap of kindness and respect between two human beings, younger and older, joining opposite worlds of East and West. In that gesture of kindness all dualism faded, dissolved. What remained strong and true was the dance of a Great Love uniting us.

Both Thomas Merton and Caryll Houselander had moments of glimpsing the true oneness of humanity. Merton was standing on a street corner in Louisville, Kentucky, when he suddenly saw the people surrounding him as a great body of life. He felt deeply and intimately connected with them in a vast oneness of spirit. A similar thing happened when the writer and artist Caryll Houselander was traveling on a crowded underground train in London. She looked around her and in her mind's eye she saw the Christ in all of them. But she saw even more than that. She had a profound sense that she was one with every person who had ever lived and ever would live, that there was an immense bond between them because of their mutual existence in time and eternity.

There are many ways to speak of the oneness that people have with all of humankind. Scientists describe this communion as the co-mingling and dancing of atoms one with another in people who are formed of the same stardust, breathe the same recycled air, and drink from the same streams of life. Christian theologians present this oneness as humanity's participation in the Body of Christ. Buddhists speak of it as the practice of compassion which views all beings as one. Native Americans approach this same oneness in their understanding of each person as their brother or sister.

Modern writers refer to this oneness as the global village. Communication today happens with amazing speed and clarity in spite of the differences in language and custom. It is less and less possible to live as isolated human beings on our planet. Yet the differences among people continue to bring division rather than harmony, to produce domination struggles and war rather than enrichment, strength, and peacefulness.

People have influenced my experience of life in many ways. They have brought me joy and gratitude, challenged my beliefs and attitudes, stretched me toward growth, and strengthened me by their welcoming presence. I close my eyes and the faces of many people I've met pass by me: ten-year-old Libby at the musical *Riverdance*, joyously balancing on the edge of her seat, cheering for the scenes she liked; a woman telling me how she sang as she gave birth to her child; two young Jewish women taking the risk to invite me to their Seder meal; the compassion-ate nurse genuinely caring about his patients; the director of a large shelter showing great respect for each homeless person; a recently widowed Italian shoe-repair man on the plane chatting away his fear of flying; being respected as a minority while I sat among a large room full of black strangers waiting to board a plane at Abidjan on the Ivory Coast.

Immigrants especially remind me of the bigger world of our diversity. The supermarket where I shop in Des Moines has almost twenty different ethnic groups represented among the personnel. I like being there mixed in with them. I draw inspiration and hope from their courage in trying to adapt to a new country, to learn the language, and to be at home amid the strangeness of it all.

Some cultures have wonderful greeting customs that easily remind them of the sacredness of the other person and of their essential unity. An Irish priest told of a tribe in Nigeria who greet one another by first touching their hand over their own heart and then extending that hand outward to the other person as an extension of their heart's love and respect. I often use the "Namaste" greeting of India as I begin a retreat or a conference talk. Namaste means, "I greet the sacred in you. I look beyond the external judgments I might make about you. I see more deeply that you are a sacred being." When we sing this to one another a significant change happens among the group. We begin to look at one another with new eyes.

The cosmic dance has helped me to recognize this sacredness in the people of my world, to view them as part of an eternal movement of love. We are one vast web of intimate connection, all sailing on the same planet, in a universe threaded with the wonder of enriching diversity.   —*Cosmic Dance*, 86–88

FULL MOON ON CHRISTMAS EVE

The heavens are telling the
glory of God.

—*Psalms 19:1a*

It is Christmas eve.
Small dry snowflakes
sing in the winter air,
a Gloria to late December.

Off we go to the country,
to my rural church
of long ago,
a choir of farming folk,
most of them quite old,
caroling from the heart
about the Babe of Bethlehem.

Their attempts at praise
bandaid my empty heart
amid a lifeless liturgy,
but what truly stirs my soul
is beyond the wooden walls.

Out in the Christmas sky
the full moon vigils,
filling snow-white cornfields
with an ethereal shine,
a steady gaze from the heavens
blessing Earth with simple beauty.

I travel in silence
among the sleepy talk,
longing to stop the car,
get out, dance awhile,
and fill my flat religion
with joy of another kind.

—*Cosmic Dance*, 54

A SMALL, SOFT FEATHER

a small, soft feather,
still warm
from bluebird's wing,
falls onto the receptive
forest floor.

lightly it lands
under a thick-branched oak;
quietly it waits,
unnoticed, unattended,

until a sister of earth pauses,
beckoned by a flutter
of unseen energy.
she bows her kindled heart

stoops ever so slowly,
and the remnant of the blue bird
comes home
to her generous hand.

days later another earth sister
opens an envelope;
resting inside, waiting,
is the blue of sky
in shape of a feather.

from warm wing
to great oak,
to earth sister
to friend,
comes the soft blue signal,

and in a sparkle of recognition
a woman, weighed down
with too many wants,
remembers how to fly.

—*Cosmic Dance*, 62

EATING TREES AND DRINKING STARS

When I was in Tucson, we had broccoli stalks for dinner. Helen
said it was like eating trees. Indeed. They do look that way. And

when I was in Colorado, Dorothy bought a bottle of champagne. As we sat sipping, she exclaimed that she was "drinking stars."

What is it about these two catchy phrases that leap like a little elf inside of me? They bring delight because they connect me with the planet and the universe. Yes, I am eating more than food and drinking more than liquid. I truly am eating trees and drinking stars. Everything is woven together in the loom of life. What feeds me has been fed by Earth. What I drink has been touched by stars. Sun has fed and nurtured grapes, those tiny beginnings of sparkle, as they matured and grew into ripeness. Moon has watched over them in the comforting shade of night, soothing these juicy fruits of vine with her tenderness.

Yes, I eat trees and I drink stars. It is a lovely thought, that one. I want to hold it near to me when I sit down to every meal. Bring on the broccoli and the champagne. It is time to hold hands with the dancing cosmos with every bite I eat and every sip I take.

THE OLD CLOSENESS

The old closeness returned
last evening.
The solitude of dusk,
the beautiful gasp of sky,
the power of the full moon,
each one embraced me.

I sat in stillness,
held close in the cleavage
of evening,
resting my longing
on her gentle bosom.

Always in those moments
I am at peace,
freed from my bones,
at one with a home

far, far away,
yet eternally close.

Who said transfiguration
is only in the scriptures?
Who said we are only
what we can prove?

They are wrong
if they speak of such things.
Last night I could prove
nothing
but I knew
everything.

—*Cosmic Dance*, 25–26

MAY I HAVE THIS DANCE?

Thus says God to these bones:
"I will cause breath to enter you,
and you shall live."

—*Ezekiel 37:5 (NRSV)*

there I am
in Ezekiel's valley,
one heap among many,
just another stack
of old, dry bones.

some Mondays
feel this way,
and Tuesdays, too,
to say nothing of
Wednesday, Thursday, Friday.

lost dreams
and forgotten pleasures,
sold like a soul
to a gluttonous world

feeding on my frenzy
and anxious activity.

but just when
the old heap of bones
seems most dry
and deserted,
a strong Breath of Life
stirs among my dead.

Someone named God
comes to my fragments
and asks, with twinkling eye:
"May I have this dance?"

the Voice stretches into me,
a stirring leaps in my heart,
lifting up the bones of death.

then I offer my waiting self
to the One who's never stopped
believing in me,
and the dance begins.

—*May I Dance*, 10–11

4

God

I am that I AM.

—Exodus 3:14

You are the deep innerness of all things,
the last word that can never be spoken.
To each of us you reveal yourself differently:
to the ship as a coastline, to the shore as a ship.

—Rainer Maria Rilke

What names or metaphors do we use in our prayer to address a God of mystery, one who is accessible and touches our hearts in both formal prayer and in unexpected moments? Does it make any difference what words we use?

—Joyce Rupp (Prayer)

Joyce Rupp grew up in Iowa with the knowledge that her purpose on earth is to know, love, and serve God, and to be happy with him in the next. As an adult who no longer found solace in some of the childhood words of her faith (1 Corinthians 13:11), Joyce found fresh power in other words that pointed in the same direction of that I AM "in whom we live and move and have our being" (Acts 17:28). Her quest for God led her to study world religions, and what she learned did not lessen but enriched her own faith. She discovered as did theologian Dorothee Solee that "There are never enough names and images for what we love."

The glimpses of oneness that first touched Joyce's heart as a child now occupied her mind. In 2011 she wrote what would become her favorite among all her books because what seemed impossible at its start flowed so easily: Fragments of Your Ancient Name, *taken from Rilke's observation that after the Fall humankind has been able only to stammer bits and pieces of the Divine One's name.*

Indeed, if Joyce were naming this chapter of this book, she might call it "The Divine One" rather than "God." I have titled it "God" because God is the name that is probably most familiar to you, and I want to draw you in at the beginning, on the contents page! The following thirty-five brief meditations from Fragments *(there are 365 in the book) clarify and expand our understanding of the many names, or qualities, of . . . the Divine One. They are taken from the scriptures of the three Abrahamic religions of Judaism, Christianity, and Islam, as well as from hymns, novels, and other literature. The name under each title refers to its source or inspiration.*

Joyce notes in her introduction that her initial fear of not being able to find 365 names was superseded by her discovery that she could have tripled that number: "While these three religions all profess belief in one divine being, each gives this being a different basic name: Yahweh, God, and Allah. I discovered that besides the Ninety-Nine Most Beautiful names of the Sufi tradition (whose listing of names varies) there is an encyclopedia of names in the Jewish mystical tradition, and in the early Syrian Christian community there were at least one hundred names for Jesus."

The last seven selections are from her book The Star in My Heart *and an article in* U.S. Catholic. *They focus on the name Sophia (Wisdom). Praying to that aspect of divinity named Sophia in the Hebrew scriptures has led Joyce to an "ever ancient, ever new" (Augustine) understanding of the only "I AM." Joyce's soul has responded with peace and gratitude to Sophia's qualities of guidance, truth-bringing, and companionship. "She is always with me as I search for the way home, which is what I am consistently doing on my spiritual path."*

Joyce's spiritual path began at home in Iowa, turned hither and yon on earth, and reached for the stars in the cosmos. How fitting that at the end of her beginning, everything comes together in the name of Wisdom.

> *Go after her and seek her:*
> *She will reveal herself to you;*
> *Once you hold her, do not let her go.*
> *For in the end you will find rest in her*
> *And she will take the form of joy in you.*
> *—Ecclesiastes 6:27–28*

GOD

Your name on the lips of human history
Has inspired but also intimidated,
Has generated truth but also falsehood,
Has strengthened but also weakened,
Has transformed but also regressed.
So many interpret you as "theirs" alone
And act for their benefit but not for yours.
In spite of such misuse and false intention,
Your name continues to motivate saints
and prosper hope when all seems lost.

Today: I accept that *God* is more than mine.
—Fragments, February 12

STEALER OF HEARTS

Hindu

You're very clever at it,
How you slip inside a prayer
Or enter a life unannounced

And claim a heart for your own.
In the flutter of an eyelid,
A long yawn or a deep breath,
Whoosh, you steal them away.
Sometimes the process is slow
But you never stop pilfering.
Come snatch my heart anytime!

Today: I give my heart willingly.

—*Fragments*, May 22

SINGER IN MY SOUL

Psalm 40:3

How resonant your presence, Singer in My Soul,
As your eloquent melodies resound in my spirit.
Each song of yours brings a message, a blessing.
The breath of your love moves through the lyrics
Captivating and enticing me away from distraction.
You are attuned to every disposition and incident.
Some days you sing loudly to awaken awareness.
At other times, you sing softly to soothe and comfort.
Whatever the cadence, the style, the libretto,
Every song of yours vibrates with unwavering love.

Today: I hear the *Singer in My Soul*.

—*Fragments*, January 26

JESUS

Matthew 1:21

Jesus, your name has been on my lips
Since I was a young and innocent child.
Now these many years since first we met
I understand you are more than a name.
To know you is to allow your teachings

To reach into the core of my daily life,
To have your vision be the vital substance
Of what truly guides and rules how I live.
How easy to bend the knee to your name
But how difficult it is to bend the heart.

Today: I make an effort to love as *Jesus* did.
—*Fragments*, January 7

THE OPENER

The Qur'an

O Divine Opener, you who free us,
There are guarded, closed-tight places
Within the deeper dimensions of self,
Places that require your assistance
So our true goodness can be liberated.
Pry apart the teeth of our stubbornness.
Swing back the door of unforgiveness.
Lift up the lid on ego-centeredness.
Knock down the walls of falseness and greed
And all that prevents oneness with you.

Today: I visit one of my places of unfreedom.
—*Fragments*, January 18

GROUND OF BEING

Paul Tillich

There is no tyranny in your divine essence.
Rather, you are part of the cause and effect
Of this intrinsic world and of our very self.
You, the solid base upon which all exists,
Remain beyond our greatest comprehension.
We can only speak about and proclaim you
Through the guiding help of symbol and story.

Still, we dare to approach and believe in you,
Because somewhere deep within our soul
We know you are who you are.

Today: I am rooted in the *Ground of Being*.
—*Fragments*, August 3

UNIFIER

Nan Merrill

We need you, divine Unifier,
To join what has broken apart
in our human relationships.
Perceived wrongs separate.
Jealousies increase hostility.
Misuse of power divides.
Selfishness easily isolates.
Disloyalty dissolves trust.
Bring us closer to one another.
Unify us in your one great heart.

Today: I move closer to those I avoid.
—*Fragments*, August 8

MY JOURNEY'S END

Karl Rahner

No one knows the precise instant
When death steals their last breath,
When the heart that beats steadily
Ceases its rhythmic functioning.
Whenever this moment arrives,
You will be ready to welcome us,
Your faithful love sweeping us away
Into another sphere of existence.
Your radiance intertwined with ours

Assuring us there is no need to fear.

Today: I place hope in *My Journey's End.*
—*Fragments*, October 20

PERPETUAL BECOMING

Jean Markale

Like a whirling dervish your love evolves,
Twirling with wonder among the cosmic void.
At the same time you encompass each soul.
Your presence expands both far and near,
Continuous motion and uninterrupted stillness
Conveying a seeming dichotomy of your being.
The fullness of your essential nature grows,
Ever enlarging as the universe stretches out.
Oh, the boundlessness of your dynamic love!
Oh, the astonishing, unlimited expansion of you!

Today: Perpetual Becoming expands in me.
—*Fragments*, January 16

JOY OF EVERY LOVING HEART

Charles Wesley

You are the gift unable to be kept secret,
Leaping out from the happiness of sharing.
You are the blessing of intentional kindness,
The sigh of satisfaction in generous giving.
You are the reward of helping hands,
The natural euphoria of each caring heart.
You are the quiet bliss of assured contentment
Coming forth from hospitable gestures.
You are the look of love in hearts that receive,
The quiet pleasure in gracious acceptance.

Today: I find *Joy* in both giving and receiving.
—*Fragments*, January 9

BECKONER

Song of Songs 2:8–12

You tap at the window of my heart.
You knock at the door of my busyness.
You call out in my night dreams.
You whisper in my haphazard prayer.
You beckon. You invite. You entice.
You woo. You holler. You insist:
"Come! Come into my waiting embrace.
Rest your turmoil in my easy silence.
Put aside your heavy bag of burdens.
Accept the simple peace I offer you."

Today: I hear and respond to the One who beckons.
—*Fragments*, February 1

DELIVERER

Psalm 18:16–19

Deliver us
From restless anxiety and impatience,
From the desire to dominate others,
From disregard for those in need,
From seeking to be the perfect one,
From destructive, gossiping words,
From immersion in selfish ambition,
From self-pity and self-doubt,
From intolerance of others' faults,
From all that attempts to destroy love.

Today: I pray for my deliverance.
—*Fragments*, March 19

LIFE

John 14:6

Like the unfolding of a fern
Or the leafing of a tree,
Like a steady mountain stream
Or strong waves of the sea,
Like a heart carrying blood
To all parts of the body,
So you are present in us.
You course through the veins
Of our souls, of our lives,
Energizing our spiritual growth.

Today: I sense *Life* pulsing in my being.

—*Fragments*, May 7

THE ONE WHO IS ALWAYS NOW

J. Philip Newell

Not even a heartbeat away from me,
You, the One who is always now, always here.
It is I who stray in thought, word, and deed.
It is I who miss the miracle of the moment.
It is I whose rhythm disregards the heartbeat
Of your steady, reassuring presence.
Each day, to renew mindfulness of you,
Each night, to deliberately turn toward you,
To you, the One Who Is Always Now,
Whose love forever beckons me to be attentive.

Today: I am attuned to the *One Who Is Always Now*.

—*Fragments*, December 30

CHILD OF BETHLEHEM

So easy to place you on a spotless pedestal,
Forgetting how you came to dwell with us,
Came, as all children come into this world,
A small babe with a bloody umbilical cord,
A wee infant nuzzling your mother's breast,
Crying out in need and filling your diapers.
How tremendous the truth of your incarnation,
Humbling yourself to vulnerable dependency.
O Child of Bethlehem, for every child alive today
Protect them in their poverty of defenselessness.

Today: I join my heart with the children of the world.
—*Fragments*, December 24

HOLY MIDWIFE

Barbara Marian

Every day a little birthing awaits us,
An opportunity pregnant with possibility.
Some of these spiritual birthings go easy.
Others are long, difficult, and agonizing.
You, Holy Midwife, attend each delivery
And urge us toward expectant growth.
Remind us that we must to do our part.
Breathe in. Breathe out. Let go. Let go.
Trust the painful contractions of labor
Preceding the precious life that follows.

Today: I listen to *Holy Midwife* urging my growth.
—*Fragments*, November 9

SACRED DARKNESS

When the desire to go forward lessens,
When the brightness of insight dims,
When the hope of finding a way fails,

It is then that I enter into your darkness
And find a nest in your sheltering womb.
Entering the hushed cave of your heart
I abide in the shadow of your presence,
Turning toward that which is not seen
But known in faith, accepted with hope.
Resting there, I am enveloped in your love.

Today: I find a secure nest in *Sacred Darkness*.
                                    —*Fragments*, December 9

VOICE IN THE FOG

Lost in thick layers of gloominess
I call out, "Where are you?"
"I'm here," you whisper back
As I strain to hear your voice.
"Are you really here?" I echo.
"Trust me," comes the response.
"But I can't see," I complain.
"Why do you need to see?"
You reply through the heavy fog,
"Is it not enough that I am here?"

Today: I listen to the *Voice in the Fog*.
                                    —*Fragments*, October 27

REFUGE FROM THE STORM

Psalm 57:1

I found needed shelter from harm
The day of the violent hailstorm
When I hurriedly sought shelter
Under the wide sycamore branches.
That stormy day reminds me of you,
The One whose canopied refuge
Spreads an eternal awning of love.
When I feel tempestuous strife

I hurry in prayer to your safe haven
And my wild storms inside do no damage.

Today: The wide branches of *Refuge* shelter me.
—*Fragments*, October 28

STORY TELLER

You never stop teaching us
Through the story of our lives
And the heritage of our world.
You continually invite us closer,
To sit on the lap of your love,
To hear your compelling narratives
And learn of our divine inheritance.
In these ageless stories we listen to
The challenging human adventure
And discover how to find our way home.

Today: I listen to the *Story Teller*.
—*Fragments*, September 16

FRIEND OF CHILDREN

Anselm Grün

You would be the last one
To snarl about a crying child
During a dignified church service.
You would be the first one
To welcome a waiting unborn
Known to have disabling features.
You would be the only one
To see deeply in a child's soul
The utter purity and radiant light
That shines on the face of angels.

Today: I resolve to be kind to every child.
—*Fragments*, August 28

MOTHER BEAR

Hosea 13:8

Do you care for us that intensely?
Do you guard us that devotedly?
Is your protection of our sacred soul
Really as ferocious as a mother bear
Safeguarding her vulnerable little ones?
If this is as the prophet Hosea states
Then why do I not value more fully
The precious gift of your loyal love?
Growl in my life every once in awhile
So I remember your affection for me.

Today: I give thanks for *Mother Bear's* affection.

—*Fragments*, August 7

OCEAN OF JOY

Kabir

Oh, that we could swim forever
In the sea of your unending joy.
Oh, that we might set happy sail
Upon the waters of your delight.
It's all close by, waiting for us
If only we stop our crazy pace
And allow our manacled calendars
To fall away from our tethered lives.
Now is the time, not later,
To let go and leap into your joy.

Today: I take the plunge.

—*Fragments*, July 25

FATHER OF THE POOR

Veni Sancte Spiritus

You provide the poorest of poor with a home,
A compassionate haven in your heart of love.
How you must long to clothe and feed them,
To visit the many disregarded and forgotten,
To comfort the countless rejected each day,
To provide the hungry what is rightfully theirs.
You look to us to be your presence for them,
To bring our skills, share our time, offer our care
In alleviating the pain of those who have little.
You ask us to join you in diminishing their poverty.

Today: I pray for commitment to those who are poor.

—*Fragments*, June 15

FORGIVER

John 8:10–11

When those who admit they have sinned
Come to you with contrite hearts,
Some easily accept your merciful welcome
While others question if it could be true.
As for myself I have sometimes wondered
If I take your forgiveness for granted,
If I go about my reckless, selfish ways
With assurance that you will absolve me.
How crucial to remember that imperative last line
I'd like to disregard: "Go now, *and sin no more*."

Today: I relate to others as one who is forgiven.

—*Fragments*, June 21

SECRET ONE

Mary Southard

Secret One, hidden in the subways
Where homeless people dwell.
Concealed in the faces of enemies
We've never met except in the news.
Disguised among our neighbors
Who rankle, offend, and annoy us.
Unnoticed in the gift of sacraments
When the eyes of our heart are veiled.
Only with the obscured view of faith
And an open spirit do we glimpse you.

Today: I look with faith for the *Secret One*.
                                        —*Fragments*, May 9

LIVING WATER

John 4:13

A rainfall of your love
Seeps into parched spirits.
A shower of your kindness
Soaks dried out caring.
A sprinkle of your grace
Moistens hardened grudges.
A stream of your comfort
Softens endless hurts.
A deluge of your peace
Washes away irritability.

Today: *Living Water* washes over me.
                                        —*Fragments*, May 4

HIDDEN ONE

Even though you are fully present
I do not always detect your nearness.
I look for you, anticipate you,
Listen for a hint of your voice
Like a tulip bulb in placid soil
Waiting for the call to rise up.
You will reveal yourself in due season.
In the meantime, I walk in faith,
Trusting you are in the heart of life,
Secreted in darkness but ever present.

Today: I have faith in divine hiddenness.

—*Fragments, April 15*

PARDONER

Karl Rahner

I have stood before you
On numerous occasions,
Knowing my transgression,
Guilty, fairly convicted.
You reach out mercifully,
Drawing my regret toward you
With a generous reception.
In that moment of pardon
The falseness in my life
Dissolves in your tenderness.

Today: I accept the divine pardon offered to me.

—*Fragments*, April 11

LORD OF THE DANCE

Sydney B. Carter

Invite me to dance.
Lead the way.
Teach me the steps
And I will follow you.
Twirl me around wildly
Or do a slow glide.
Whatever the form
I will remain in step,
Heeding the gestures
Of your graced movement.

Today: I let the *Lord of the Dance* lead me.
—*Fragments*, April 10

CORE OF COMMUNITY

Acts 2:43–47

With you as the nucleus
Of every group that gathers,
Differences are respected
And tensions are overcome.
Those speaking from the edge
Gain a listening ear.
Compassion thrives.
Egos maintain a low profile.
With you as Core of Community
Peace abides and love abounds.

Today: The *Core of Community* affects my
relationships.
—*Fragments*, March 21

GOD WHO BREAKS CHAINS

Elizabeth Johnson

I have been bound time and again
By fetters that shackled me tightly
And entangled my heart's desires.
These countless, vapid excuses of mine
For not being the person I could be
Have restrained the love in my heart
Intended to flow outward to others.
You continually show me these chains
And help me break loose, to be free
From whatever chokes my goodness.

Today: I pay attention to what chains me.

—*Fragments*, March 7

FRIEND OF THE POOR

The poor are everywhere,
Those society rejects or forgets.
You welcome them all.
You look toward. I look away.
You reach out. I hold back.
You accept fondly. I rebuff fearfully.
You give away. I clutch tightly.
You extend love. I offer pity.
When will I, too, go in your direction
And become a friend of the poor?

Today: I befriend those I reject or forget.

—*Fragments*, February 23

SACRED SOURCE OF SLEEP

Edward Hays

Sleep, glorious sleep, mysterious sleep!
How remarkable that nightly moment
When sleep overtakes our consciousness
And slips us through the sleeve of rest,
When dreams arise to reach and teach,
And angels wrap their wings around us.
For all those nights and naps I've slept
As sweet and soundly as a contented baby,
Thank you, Sacred Source of Sleep,
For rest and renewal of body and spirit.

Today: Before I fall asleep, I give thanks for this
gift.

—*Fragments*, February 20

SOPHIA

Proverbs 8:1

Sophia, whose name in Greek means "wisdom,"
You provide a welcome, refreshing respite
For those seeking a feminine view of divinity.
Yet, some seekers shun and even condemn you.
Others think your beautiful name is a sham.
How could a personage so enticingly alive
Be the cause for disturbing, cataclysmic concern?
Your wisdom is truly our spiritual wealth.
Your dynamic presence offers the purest guidance.
Thank you, Sophia, for the gifts you contain.

Today: I call on *Sophia* to guide me in her ways.

—*Fragments*, January 21

In her introduction to The Star in My Heart, *a book on the healing images of Feminine Wisdom in the Hebrew scriptures, Joyce tells us how the book was born on a sunny day when she was watching a two-year-old girl "playing among the flowers, talking to them, laughing, and splashing the roses with her little watering can.*

"It was there that I became keenly aware of Sophia's presence. I looked at the beautiful child at play, and I remembered how Sophia (Wisdom) speaks of herself in Proverbs:

> *"'I was at God's side . . . delighting God day after day, ever at play in God's presence, at play everywhere in God's world.'"*
>
> — *Proverbs 8:30–31*

The following selections are first an essay that Joyce wrote for U.S. Catholic *that sums up her learnings on Sophia, and then readings from* The Star in My Heart.

SOPHIA: A LOST BIBLICAL TREASURE

At a retreat where I referred to Sophia several times in my first presentation, a man suddenly stood up and blurted out: "Just who is this Sophia? Stop assuming that everyone here knows who you are talking about!" His interruption startled me but it was also a gift. He helped me lower my expectations about Sophia being readily known and loved. His question reminded me that many do not know this jewel in the scriptures who is hidden not only from men, but from women as well.

His question was also a challenge because I knew that introducing Sophia would take awhile to do. There is so much of this lost heritage to recover. Fortunately, he had the willingness to stay for the whole weekend so we had time to talk about his question. I found him open, ready to learn and to grow. As we departed from the retreat the two of us had a new appreciation for one another and for the gift of Sophia. He left with gratitude for discovering a new way of relating to the Holy One. I left with thanks for his query because it led me to renewed appreciation for the journey I have traveled with Sophia.

As I spoke about Sophia I reflected back to thirteen years earlier when I had received a letter one spring day from a publisher asking me to contribute a book to their women's series. I wanted to say "yes" but I was blank as to what I might write. It took me four months and an amazing intuitive event before I responded to that letter. The unexpected moment came while I was caring for my friends' two year old daughter. We were out in the rose garden where I was enjoying the happy child as she danced around the flowers, singing with glee. While I watched Elizabeth playing, something stirred in me and I found myself reaching for pen and paper.

Although I did not comprehend this stirring at the time, I found myself writing a book proposal based on the theme of something that had enticed me time and again: my attraction to wisdom in the scriptures. My book proposal was very sketchy. At that time I had very little knowledge of the biblical books of wisdom and I definitely did not know that in the Greek translation the words for Holy Wisdom are "Hagia Sophia." I also had no awareness that this Sophia would offer me a fresh and deeply profound way of relating to the divine.

Only much later did I realize that the image of little Elizabeth playing among the roses was reflective of the beautiful passage in Proverbs 8 in which Sophia is described as being present at the beginning of creation: "When there were no depths I was brought forth . . . when God established the heavens I was there . . . playing before (God) all the while . . ." (v. 24, 30). It was this connection with Proverbs that elicited my desire to explore and write about wisdom while I watched the young child playing amid the flowers.

That surprising moment was the beginning of a long and wonderful journey of exploration and research. When my proposal for the book was accepted, I took a deep gulp and asked myself: "Just what, or who, is this beautiful figure that Proverbs describes as a partner with the Holy One?"

Divine Wisdom as "She"

I began my exploration and research by reading and meditating each day on one of the scripture passages referring to Holy Wisdom. As I prayed, I noticed how Sophia was always referred to as "she." This amazed me even though I knew there were many ways to describe and relate to God. I believed the poet William Blake's observation that "all deities reside in the human breast." I knew that God was neither male nor female, yet I also knew God to be consistently described as "male" and referred to as "he" in Christian images and metaphors. Feminine pronouns and figures have rarely been used in speaking of God, even though, as I discovered, there are numerous references in the wisdom literature to Divine Wisdom as "she" and plenty of feminine qualities to describe "her."

Many people think of wisdom as an "it" rather than a "she." Actually, both of these approaches are accurate because there are two types of wisdom present in the Bible. Some passages speak of wisdom as a quality or a truth to guide our lives. Here wisdom is presented as a "thing"—such as wise sayings, proverbs, and moral exhortations. There are many other passages, however, that refer to wisdom as a person. It is here that the feminine pronoun is always used and is consistently reflective of the divine presence. This wisdom is Holy Wisdom: Hagia Sophia.

Historically, the authors of the wisdom literature began this feminine reference to Sophia within 33 BCE and 4–5 CE. There are only four other figures who are mentioned more than Sophia in the Jewish scriptures (the "Old Testament"): Yahweh, Moses, David, and Job. Given this fact, it is quite incredible that so few know much about her. However, I do understand why she has not been recognized because I, too, had a difficult time discovering and claiming her.

I asked a friend who taught religious studies at a local university to read my manuscript. When she returned it to me, she queried: "Well, is Sophia divine or not?" I blanched when she said that because I still did not know after almost two years of prayer and study of the biblical passages, if the references were simply personified metaphors for divinity or if Sophia was truly another word for the radiant presence of the Holy One. I was scared to respond: "Yes, I think she is more than metaphor; she *is* an expression of the presence of God." I still wasn't sure and I didn't want to lead anyone astray. It took another year for me to be convinced that both "Sophia" and "God" were the same names for divinity.

During that year, one of the marvelous descriptions of Sophia that convinced me I was not off on some heretical tangent was discovering what Thomas Merton wrote about her in *Emblems of a Season of Fury*: "The Diffuse Shining of God is Hagia Sophia . . . Sophia is Gift, is Spirit, Donum Dei. She is God-given and God Himself as Gift . . . Sophia in all things is the Divine Life reflected in them" (pp. 509–510).

Another confirmation was seeing how the Book of Wisdom describes Sophia guiding the Exodus people through the wilderness: "She led them by a marvelous road. She herself was their shelter by day and their starlight through the night" (Ws 10:17). This passage was clearly another way of speaking about the faithful God who "went in front of them in a pillar of cloud by day...and a pillar of fire by night" (Ex 13:21). I was finally convinced that Sophia was truly another way of naming the divine.

How the Treasure of Sophia Got Lost

Historically, Sophia was not always hidden. There are at least three major reasons why this treasure has been missing from our spiritual heritage. The early Church knew Sophia well and prayed to her. However, many Greek and Egyptian goddess cults still existed at this time and there was growing concern among Christians that worship of Sophia would be associated with these cults. Some of the qualities ascribed to the goddesses were similar to Sophia's attributes, particularly those of the Egyptian goddess, Isis, who was renowned for her wisdom and guidance. Fear of the goddesses was one reason why the early Roman church gradually disconnected from Sophia.

Concurrent with this situation was the rise of gnosticsm, an early Christian movement whose followers had special devotion to Sophia, crediting her with the creation of the universe. The Gnostics had an immense longing for the interior life and for the hidden things of God. Eventually they were charged with heresy, not because of their love for Sophia, but because they rejected the material world. In their passion for the interior life, the Gnostics accepted only the value of the spiritual and intellectual realms. They taught that Jesus was never incarnated, that salvation was to be attained only through knowledge of the inner self. This left the early Church in a bind; they believed in Sophia yet rejected Gnosticism. As the Church distanced itself from the Gnostics, it also turned away from devotion to Sophia for fear of approving Gnostic beliefs.

A third development leading to the loss of Sophia was the theology of first century philosopher, Philo of Alexander. As a Jew, Philo was very familiar with Sophia. He taught that the Divine Origin (Yahweh) had created Sophia first and then, Logos (the Word) as a balancing companion. He envisioned these two working together in shaping creation: Sophia, the feminine or creating vessel, and Logos, the masculine or active doer. There are various theories as to how Sophia was eventually left out of Philo's approach. Some historians say it became difficult in his work to separate the Logos from Sophia, so gradually only the aspect of Logos was kept. Others say it was a strong patriarchal emphasis on the masculine that caused the feminine to be eliminated.

For a time the early Church referred to Sophia in terms comparable to that of the Holy Spirit but this, too, gradually diminished and was lost. Whatever happened, one thing is clear: there are striking parallels between the attributes of Sophia and the qualities of Jesus. There is much about Jesus that is like Sophia.

In the Jewish scriptures, Sophia is a feminine voice, in contrast to a God of dominion and force. Jesus, too, has a Sophia heart, not the heart of someone seeking power. Sophia is concealed but ready to reveal just as Jesus is "the hidden wisdom of

God" (1 Cor 2:7), "the revelation of the mystery kept secret for endless ages"(Rom 16:25). Both Sophia and Jesus are brought forth by God and both are sent by God to be special messengers to humanity, bringing wisdom, counsel and guidance. Each is a healer and a comforter, a messenger of truth, perception, and guidance. Both are teachers who instruct in the ways of God and both are referred to as "light."

Sophia as a Spiritual Treasure

I have come to know and love Sophia. The qualities attributed to her in the various wisdom passages have greatly influenced my spiritual life. I will never be the same because of her. That is why I resonated so much when a participant at a workshop asked: "Could you speak about Sophia? My spiritual director introduced me to her a few years ago and this has changed my life." I wanted to walk right over and hug that man because his question gave me an opportunity to talk about the beautiful gifts for spiritual growth that Holy Wisdom offers to those who seek her.

The Book of Wisdom (often attributed to the wise King Solomon but actually authored by an unknown writer) has many beautiful passages about Sophia. In chapter 7 she is described as being "the breath of the power of God, a pure emanation of the glory of the Almighty . . . a reflection of eternal light, a spotless mirror of the working of God and an image of (God's) goodness" (Wis 7:25–27). One could spend a year just pondering this chapter with its rich presentation of Sophia as a radiant, indwelling presence shining in our midst.

Sophia has depth and is full of mystery. While she is "readily seen by those who seek her" (Wis 6:12; Sir 6:27) and is as near as our next breath, she is equally full of mystery and needs to be discovered: "Happy is the person who meditates on Sophia . . . who reflects in one's heart on Sophia's ways and ponders her secrets, pursuing her like a hunter, and lying in wait on her paths" (Sir 15:20–22).

Attentiveness and alertness are essential in order to find Sophia. Both Proverbs and the Book of Wisdom present Sophia as sitting by the city gates, crying out at the busiest corners by the entrance to the city" (Wis 6:14; Prov 1:20–21). The gates of biblical times were the entrance into the marketplace or heart of the city. Symbolically, the gates where we meet Sophia today are in the midst of our busy, marketplace lives. It is here that we can still discover Divine Wisdom, who is always ready to guide and direct our lives if we are aware of and open to her.

There are many other metaphors for Sophia. She is a teacher: "Hear for I will speak noble things. Take my instruction" (Prov 8:1–11); a mother: "She brings up her own children" (Sir 4:11–18); "the tree of life" (Prov 3:8, Wis 10:17–19, Sir 14:20–27), and true wealth: "more precious than jewels" (Prov 3:15). She is also described as a counselor, a fine mist, light, and the law. Sophia provides healing and shelter, gives rest, and offers what is needed for spiritual transformation.

I count on Sophia to influence my attitudes, values and beliefs; to help me make good choices and decisions. I pray to her each day to guide me as I try to reflect her love in all I am and all I do. Whenever I am in doubt as to how to proceed in my work and relationships I turn to Sophia for wisdom and courage. She has never failed to be there for me.

Finding the Treasure

One day as I concluded a talk on Sophia, a woman queried: "You told us how Sophia got lost. Now tell us: How do we find her?" I suggested that she begin by reading, studying, and meditating on the Sophia passages in the Bible and that she take a metaphor or a name for Sophia in the verses, breathe it in and out, letting it permeate her whole being. "Most essential of all," I responded, "is to ask Sophia to reveal herself to you."

We need to look for Sophia. By her very nature she is relational, present in the world, interacting among people and ordinary human lives. By desiring to know her, by opening our minds and hearts, her radiance will permeate our lives. Such is what happened with a concerned mother recently. She was having much difficulty with her two young daughters who were sulky and disruptive. One day after work she sat alone in her car feeling sad and troubled. She called on Sophia for guidance and insight, praying quietly for some time. Then she drove home, sat down with her daughters and together they came to some much needed household compromises that made all of them more peaceful and happy.

Prayer is vital in discovering the treasure of Sophia. This helped me the most in finding her and establishing a faithful relationship. I believe it is time for Christians to recover the richness of this heritage of the divine feminine that has been lost. We need Sophia now, more than ever. We need her compassionate presence and her ability to help us see clearly in the midst of a world that cries out for wisdom and love. Sophia will not fail us. She will always draw us deeper and further for there is no end to the mystery of her life with us. "The first person did not finish discovering about her nor has the most recent tracked her down; for her thoughts are wider than the sea, and her designs more profound than the abyss" (Sir 24:28–29).   —U.S. Catholic

MY JOURNEY TO SOPHIA

This book, *The Star in My Heart*, was born on a sunny day as I sat among the myriad colors and fragrances of my friends' rose garden. I was watching over their two-year-old, Elizabeth Ann, who was delightfully playing among the flowers, talking to them, laughing, and splashing the roses with her little watering can. It was there that I became keenly aware of Sophia's presence. I looked at the beautiful child at play, and I remembered how Sophia (Wisdom) speaks of herself in Proverbs:

> *I was at God's side . . . delighting God day after day, ever at play in God's presence, at play everywhere in God's world . . .*
>
> —*Proverbs 8:30–31*

It was not the first time that I had experienced this deep awareness of Sophia's presence. There had been many moments in my life when the sudden recognition of her radiant presence had pressed tears into my eyes. Oftentimes it happened when I looked upon something in nature and felt a wordless connection between the vast beauty of the universe and the goodness of Divine life.

This kind of recognition happened when I saw Elizabeth at play. In an instant all the years that stretched between Elizabeth's age and my own were connected. I saw how Sophia had touched my heart time and again and had brought me to truths that had indeed changed my life. I knew then that I wanted to write about Sophia's presence in my life. I wanted to tell how her activity in my spirit has led me to many truths which now inspire my life's journey and give order to my inner being.

For many years I have had a file folder labeled "wisdom." It began by my being intrigued with the wisdom literature of the Hebrew scriptures. I found many verses there that connected to my own story. In the poetry of those scriptures, Wisdom is referred to as "she," a rather exceptional event in a strongly male-dominated world. In many cultures of the past, including Egyptian, Babylonian, and Chinese, wisdom was considered to be something very practical, a means of moral values as well as of right living which is given in maxims and proverbs. In the Hebrew scriptures wisdom is also associated with guidance, but there is a wonderful addition: Wisdom becomes alive. Wisdom becomes a person, a "she." This feminine wisdom is presented as one who not only gives us direction for our lives but is intimately bonded with God. She is a breath of the Divine, born before creation; her origin contains great mystery. She is given to humankind to connect them with the Divine. Wisdom is a unique manifestation of God, a catalyst for transformation of the human person's life into one of light and goodness. This is the way she is described in the book of Wisdom:

> *Within her is a spirit intelligent, holy,*
> *unique, manifold, subtle,*
> *active, incisive, unsullied,*
> *lucid, invulnerable, benevolent,*
> *sharp, irresistible, beneficent, loving to humankind,*

steadfast, dependable, unperturbed,
almighty, all-surveying,
penetrating all intelligent, pure,
and most subtle spirits;
for Wisdom is quicker to move than any motion;
she is so pure, she pervades and permeates all things.
She is a breath of the power of God,
pure emanation of the glory of the Almighty;
hence nothing impure can find a way into her.
She is a reflection of the eternal light,
untarnished mirror of God's active power,
image of God's goodness.

—*Wisdom* 7:22–26
—*Sophia*, 1–3

THE OWL GAZED BACK AT ME

It was a mystical morning. There was a quiet mist and a gentle fog that shrouded the woods with an inviting veil of silence. It was in this contemplative moment that I met the owl. My heart leapt as I looked up and saw it sitting there on top of a road sign, just a few feet in front of me. I stopped instantly and gazed in disbelief at what I saw. The owl gazed back at me. I had never been so close to an owl. I stood there for a long time, absorbed in the silence and the beauty of the bird. The owl never moved, but the eyes were focused on me. I felt a tremendous drawing to that silent figure. Something in me yearned to touch the soft feathers, to draw nearer to those large round eyes. Finally I took a small step toward the owl, and just that quickly the wide-winged bird lifted off silently and flew away.

I was not disappointed. I knew I could not stand there all day looking at an owl. I also knew the owl would probably not sit there all day looking at me. It had to come to an end. But all day long my heart sang in memory of seeing the owl. It sang the next day and the next. At times I would say to myself, "Did I really see that owl? Was I really that close?" And then I would sense all over again the tremendous drawing power of that moment. I will never forget the communion I felt in that simple, unexpected meeting of the owl. Since then I have often heard an owl's hoot in the late night or early morning. Whenever I have heard it, I have been immediately connected with the experience of that mystical October morning.

Was it mere coincidence that I should meet an owl as I began to write about Sophia? I do not know. I only know that the owl's presence became a special symbol for me as I wrote the pages of this book (*The Star in My Heart*). The fears about what I would write left me after I met the owl. A sense of urgency filled me. I concentrated on the power of my unexpected meetings with Sophia. I could not wait to see what I would discover about Sophia as I pondered her presence in my life. I was constantly amazed. What I have discovered is that my meeting with Sophia has been as strong and as real as my meeting with the owl—and just as elusive. —*Star*, 88–93

THE STAR IN MY HEART

Wisdom is bright and does not grow dim. By
those who love her she is readily seen, and
found by those who look for her.
—*Wisdom 6:12*

Sophia, to you I come:
you are the Wisdom of God
you are the Whirl of the Spirit
you are the Intimate Connection
you are the Star in my Heart
Sophia,
open my being to the radiance of your presence
to the guidance of your companionship
to the compassion of your indwelling
to the lighting of your blessed vision
Sophia,
trusted friend, beloved companion,

Sophia,
mercy-maker, truth-bearer, love-dweller,
Sophia,
all goodness resides within you.
Sophia,
take me by the hand
bless the frailty of my weak places
strengthen my ability to dwell in darkness
for it is there that your deepest secrets are revealed.
Sophia,
we walk together!

The stars have long been earth companions for me. Since I was a child I have looked at the night skies and loved what I saw there. Something about the stars radiates hope in my heart and draws me far beyond my little space of earth. An old family friend told me that one evening he and his wife had come to visit my mother and father after we children were all safely tucked into bed. Late in the evening they heard a rustle in the kitchen, and they found me standing by the window. When they asked me why I wasn't in bed, I said very plainly in my three-year-old voice, "Oh, I just wanted to come down and look at the stars." Hearing this story made me wonder if my love of the stars was perhaps born at that very early age. It certainly confirmed my deep connection with these radiant friends of the universe.

As an adult I have kept my fondness for the stars and feel a special leap of delight when I pause in a wintry evening to see the strong and bold marks of Orion in the sky. Or on a summer's night, to walk along and gaze up at the community of light in the Pleiades. I feel that the stars bless me with their presence. There have been times in the midst of deep pain in my heart that I have walked under the night sky and cried out to God, "By the light of your stars, heal me." There is something extremely consoling about walking in great darkness and having the light of the stars to guide the way. After a walk under the stars, light eventually returns to my darkened spirit. The healing that I need comes in future days (or months!) through people, books, sacred moments, music, insights, all of which clarify my confusion and soften the pain in my heart.

I like to think of Sophia as a star in my heart, one whose light guides me and consoles me in my inner darkness, drawing me to a bondedness with a greater truth than I presently know or understand. No matter how hard I fight to stay "in the light," I will have some darkness in my life. This is as sure as the pattern of sunrise and sunset in the natural course of the day. My darkness comes from many sources, sometimes from the pain and struggle of changing ideas, relationships or work, or from my participation in the human condition of aging, accidents, and illness. It has also come from that silent journey when I have desired to be more united with the Divine who is the beloved one dwelling at the center of who I am. This calls for the risky journey into the depths of myself because, most often, the way to the Divine is one of going through the passage of darkness within, having only the glimmer of Sophia's light to tend the way.

The Divine is also discovered in my happy, joyous, light-filled times, but no matter how much light I carry within me, there will always be times of feeling lost, being confused, seeking direction. It is the way of the human heart. It is the way of going inward. It is the way of Sophia.

At times I have found it difficult to believe that darkness could be a source of growth. Darkness to a child, as well as to many adults, can be a scary, fearsome place where wild creatures wait to pounce and prey. But, in actuality, some kinds of darkness are truly our friends. The world of our mother's womb had no light: It is where we grew wonderfully and filled out our tiny limbs of life. Our earth would be quite lifeless, too, if we did not plant seeds deep within the lonely darkness of the soil so they could germinate and bring forth green shoots. I know, too, that we would soon die of an overheated planet if nightfall did not come to soothe the sun-filled land. Darkness is very essential for some aspects of growth and protection.

But there is also an unfriendly darkness, like human destructiveness or hate, a blackness that can maim and wound us mentally, emotionally, spiritually. It is the kind that will lead us to despair, where we end up hurting ourselves or others. It destroys our hope and our positive view of life. We do not grow in this kind of darkness. We turn in on self. We stop believing in our goodness and beauty and that of others.

How do I know what kind of darkness to stay in? It is not easy to know. Sometimes I just do not know. I always need someone to walk faithfully with me during these times of darkness. Sophia's light and guidance are present to me through my human companions. A spiritual guide or a counseling companion is a great blessing at such a time. If at all possible, I need to find these people and welcome them into my life. If I call on Sophia, she will lead me to these companions.

I will need to wait the darkness out, say it out, pray it out. Eventually, I will know what kind of darkness it is by the effects that it has on my life and on the lives of those around me. If it brings life (new hope, greater understanding, more courage, deeper trust . . .), the darkness is my friend. I believe that almost all of my darkness is life-giving if I have Sophia with me. Jessica Powers understood this when she wrote: "God sits on a chair of darkness in my soul." Sophia is my Star to light up what seems to be an unbearable or impossible passage of life. I may not want to believe that darkness can be growthful because ache, loneliness, hurt, hollowness are not feelings that I enjoy. Yet, if I look back on my life, to those dark times, I can see that I have, or could have, grown deeper and wiser from my experience of the darkness.   —*Star*, xxx–5

THE DARKNESS WAS GOOD FOR ME

I remember a passageway in my life, years ago, when I was far from home for the first time. I lived with people I did not know. I taught school in a place I did not like. I felt a tremendous loneliness like a black cloud over me day after day. I felt sad and empty all the time. I could not imagine how this darkness would be good for me. All I wanted to do was to run away from it. But I had accepted a teaching position, and I felt a responsibility to stay.

This experience ended up being one of the best things that ever happened to me. I call those years of loneliness my "island years" because it was then that I learned to live with myself. After several months of intense sadness, something in me nudged me to go to the woods regularly to ponder life. At first when I went there, I felt only my loneliness. Eventually I began to learn from it. My loneliness was saying to me, "Spend time with yourself. Don't run away." I began to see how afraid I was of myself, how fearful I was to look inside. As I was drawn to go within, I discovered, to my great surprise, that there was goodness and beauty there. I learned, too, that I was not alone. I began sensing the companionship of God dwelling within me. I did not know Sophia then, but now I see that it was she who guided me during that dark time. It was she who led me through my fears and loneliness. It was Sophia who held my hand and drew me to her light within me.

There is a story told in the Christian scriptures of three astrologers who followed an immensely bright star (Matthew 2:1–12). They were so drawn by this star that they followed a hunch in their hearts that it would lead them to the Divine. So set were their hearts on this bright vision in the sky that they pursued it over great distances and through many struggles. Following the star meant that they had to do their traveling at night. They did not know where they would be led. They only knew that they had to follow. They lost sight of the star, and in great humility, they had to rely on other star-seekers to tell them where to locate the star again.

This star "filled their hearts with delight" (Matthew 2:10). They continued to follow it in the darkness of the night, journeying until finally they found themselves at the feet of the one whom they had long sought. Surely Sophia must have danced a radiant star dance on that night when these weary travelers finally reached the goal of their long journey.

This story is so like my own inner one. I feel drawn to seek the Divine. I go mostly in the night, not being sure of the direction, or of what this God will look like, or where the journey will take me. I lose my way. Then I find others who have seen the star. They show me and guide me. I find the way again. And one day I discover God as the beloved, the one for whom I have so yearned. This may be in the most unlikely of places, and perhaps just for a fleeting moment, but I know in that brief discovery that the journey has been worth it. My heart, like those seekers of long ago, is filled with delight. This discovery is usually a very brief experience. And so I continue on the journey of life with hope in my heart, seeking by the light of the star to have another glimpse of the beloved.

This is the way of those who choose to know Sophia and to pursue her secrets, the secrets of wisdom that lead to wholeness of life, to peace of heart.

I love the Star in my heart. She has taken my hand so often and has led me through the dark times. I believe that she is a companion through the darkness for all of us. She helps us to not be so afraid and to trust in our journey to the inner places which we have yet to visit. It is good for us to remember this truth in our dark times, for Sophia is *"bright and does not grow dim. By those who love her she is readily seen, and found by those who look for her"* (Wisdom 6:12).

Here are some of the wisdoms I am finding with Sophia's guidance:

- *Solitude* and *reflection* are essential for my inward journey, but I also need *others* to help me walk through the fearsome tunnels of darkness.
- In the seasons of my inner life, Sophia's presence can soften the anguish or isolation of the darkness, but she will not take it away from me. The darkness is necessary for my *growth*.

- My fears and anxieties can quietly, or noisily, tend to take over my decisions and my choices if there is no *awareness* of them, sapping me of my energy for life-giving experiences.
- If I stay in the *darkness* long enough, my eyes become more accustomed to the dark, and I begin to see things of *beauty* and *freedom* that I never knew were present.

Meeting Sophia

1. Take time with the stars. Sit under them. Walk with them. Let yourself dance with them. Be with these friends of the universe and let them speak to you of the journey in your heart.

2. Reflect upon the Star in your heart.

Relax your body/mind/spirit. See yourself in a place of beauty somewhere away from the city. Use your senses to become a part of your environment. Notice how the air smells, what you hear. Sit down and feel the earth or sand or rock or . . . Be attentive to all that you can see around you.

Dusk slowly comes to the place where you are sitting. Be with the sunset, the fading hot, the darkness as it quietly descends upon you. See yourself sitting now in the darkness. Look up and see that the first star of the evening has come. Continue to look and see how the sky gradually fills with a brilliant, star-filled expanse. Everywhere you look there are stars sparkling and glowing.

Focus on one star. See it slowly fall from the sky. It glides toward you in a welcoming way. It comes closer. Quietly, tenderly, it falls into your heart. It does so with great ease and comfort. It does not burn or harm. It only glows with peaceful light. See the star shining there for you. Rest in peace with the star. Speak to the star. Let the star speak to you. Continue to be with the star until you are both silent again. Gradually return to the daylight.

Take some time to write or draw or paint your response to this meeting of the Star in your heart. You might also consider using clay to complete this experience of the Star within you. Let the clay speak of the Star falling into your heart.

3. Reflect on your own wisdoms regarding the Star in your heart. How have you experienced darkness? What do you know of Sophia's presence in your darkness? What do you believe about your life's journey of darkness and light? Write these discovered wisdoms in your journal.

4. Try drawing a mandala, a sacred circle. Fill it with symbols or words that describe the light and the dark within you. Let yourself enter into this sacred image. After this "entering in," write a prayer to Sophia.   —*Star*, 5–10

FAR-SEEING EYES

She is so pure,
she pervades and permeates all things.
—*Wisdom* 7:24

I have long yearned to be a far-seeing person. Sometimes this yearning has been granted to me, although I am often one of those who hurries through the day, missing the inner connections, and falls into bed at night with no inner vision. But when the far-seeing moments come, they are a wondrous gift. I often find these moments recorded in my journal. Life moves so fast that I can easily forget they have happened to me unless I take time to record them. When I go back and read my journal, I am astounded at how much Sophia has blessed me.

One far-seeing moment was that of a very foggy morning when I arose to greet the God of dawn. The retreat center where I was staying had a small pond nearby that was surrounded by Scotch pines. As I awoke, I felt called by Sophia to go and sit on the white swing near the pond, to simply be present to the mystery before me.

As I sat there, enveloped by the wet world, the mist rose wonderfully from the pond. At times it lifted so high that the trees were clearly reflected in the water's eye. Then their images would quickly disappear with another big breath of misty air covering the pond. I felt myself becoming one with all that was there, one with the mist rising and moving, coming and going; one with the ducks preening and chewing; one with the mourning doves murmuring and cooing. I was serenely connected to the whole scene. The air over the pond cleared one more time, and the pines were again etched on the face of the water. Tears came to my eyes as I recognized my own story there, a midlife one of losing my dreams and finding them again, over and over, an alternating series of blurred vision and vibrant clarity much like the image of the trees in the misty pond. I felt greatly comforted by the pond that morning. It assured me that my inner journey was a natural part of my adult growth.

Another such experience happened to me as I went for a walk one February morning in early dawn. It was a cold wintry Midwest day, and a quiet snow was falling. There was just enough white on the ground that I could see my footprints very clearly as I stopped to relish the beauty of the snowfall. I continued my walk among the gentle snowflakes and then turned around to come home. As I approached the place where I had stopped earlier, I saw that in less than thirty minutes my footprints had disappeared, completely covered by the newly fallen snow. Something inside of me was astounded by this fact. I hurried on home and prepared for work.

As I went through the day, I kept finding the image of my "erased footprints" in my mind. That evening Sophia called to me to not let that event go without some reflection, so I sat down to be with the footprints. Then it came to me so clearly: How very quickly my life will be gone. I think of my life as vital and significant, yet I am so small and so insignificant in such a vast world. I saw how fleeting life is and how much I do treasure the gift of it. It was humbling to recognize this. The words of Psalm 90 came to me: "Teach us to count how few days we have and so gain wisdom of heart" (Psalm 90:12). Again, this

gift of Sophia, this far-seeing moment, gave me a vision to keep
in my heart forever, a vision to influence the way I walk through
my days.

—*Star*, 12–17

MY JOURNEY TO WISDOM

Once upon a time
a child of happiness danced upon the land,
knew friendship with the earth
and celebrated life
with her love of solitude and simple things.

She grew into a young woman,
whose vision of self was clouded,
clothed with the complexities of insecurity
and the necessity of leaving the hallowed womb
of the quiet earth.

She walked into cities of strangers,
straining her inner eye to catch
the slightest hint of the beauty
that had energized her younger days
when she played upon the earth.

Days stretched into months
and then years went by.
She slowly changed by going deeper,
deeper, into her Center.
Never understanding why the desire
to go deeper was there
but always knowing there was no other choice
than to follow at all cost.
Darkness often loomed up large
against her searching journey.
Risk and Truth became her companions.

She met Compassion
and then Wisdom came to greet her.
So close, at times, were these companions
that she wept for their intensity
and her unworthiness.
Still, they walked with her,
and everywhere she went
her companions reached out
and blessed the people of her life.

She could only kneel in gratitude,
offering her heart of praise
to the Divine Companion
who had faithfully kept the kindling of love
burning in her heart.

—*Star*, xx–xxi

MODERN SPIRITUAL MASTERS
Robert Ellsberg, Series Editor

*This series introduces the essential writing and vision of some
of the great spiritual teachers of our time. While many of these
figures are rooted in long-established traditions of spirituality,
others have charted new, untested paths. In each case, however,
they have engaged in a spiritual journey shaped by the challenges
and concerns of our age. Together with the saints and witnesses
of previous centuries, these modern spiritual masters may serve
as guides and companions to a new generation of seekers.*

Etty Hillesum (edited by Annemarie S. Kidder)
Caryll Houselander (edited by Wendy M. Wright)
Pope John XXIII (edited by Jean Maalouf)
Rufus Jones (edited by Kerry Walters)
Clarence Jordan (edited by Joyce Hollyday)
Walter Kasper (edited by Patricia C. Bellm and Robert A. Krieg)
John Main (edited by Laurence Freeman)
James Martin (edited by James T. Keane)
Anthony de Mello (edited by William Dych, S.J.)
Thomas Merton (edited by Christine M. Bochen)
John Muir (edited by Tim Flinders)
John Henry Newman (edited by John T. Ford, C.S.C.)
Henri Nouwen (edited by Robert A. Jonas)
Flannery O'Connor (edited by Robert Ellsberg)
Karl Rahner (edited by Philip Endean)
Brother Roger of Taizé (edited by Marcello Fidanzio)
Oscar Romero (by Marie Dennis, Rennie Golden, and Scott
    Wright)
Joyce Rupp (edited by Michael Leach)
Albert Schweitzer (edited by James Brabazon)
Frank Sheed and Maisie Ward (edited by David Meconi)
Sadhu Sundar Singh (edited by Charles E. Moore)
Mother Maria Skobtsova (introduction by Jim Forest)
Dorothee Soelle (edited by Dianne L. Oliver)
Edith Stein (edited by John Sullivan, O.C.D.)
David Steindl-Rast (edited by Clare Hallward)
William Stringfellow (edited by Bill Wylie-Kellerman)
Pierre Teilhard de Chardin (edited by Ursula King)
Mother Teresa (edited by Jean Maalouf)
St. Thérèse of Lisieux (edited by Mary Frohlich)
Phyllis Tickle (edited by Jon M. Sweeney)
Henry David Thoreau (edited by Tim Flinders)
Howard Thurman (edited by Mary Krohlich)
Leo Tolstoy (edited by Charles E. Moore)
Evelyn Underhill (edited by Emilie Griffin)
Vincent Van Gogh (by Carol Berry)
Jean Vanier (edited by Carolyn Whitney-Brown)
Swami Vivekananda (edited by Victor M. Parachin)
Simone Weil (edited by Eric O. Springsted)
John Howard Yoder (edited by Paul Martens and Jenny Howells)